The Crisis Leader

The Art of Leadership in Times of Crisis

Gisli Olafsson

The Crisis Leader: The Art of Leadership in Times of Crisis
Gisli Rafn Olafsson

Copyeditors: Susanne Jul and Kristin Milburn Smith
Cover Design: Axel Örn Gíslason

Published in the United States by Lorien Consulting

Dedication

To my children, Theodora Angel, Ólafur Rafn, Chastity Rose, Axel Örn, and Katla Maria - the best children any father could wish for!

To my wife, Sonja Dögg - the love of my life and the rock I cling to!

About the Author

To learn how to deal with a crisis, try being the parent of five teenagers!

Gisli Olafsson

Gisli Olafsson is one of the leading experts in the world on the use of technology in disaster response. He is a sought after speaker, trainer, and advisor on the role information technology can play in enhancing the responses to large-scale natural and man-made disasters. After starting out as a search and rescue volunteer almost two decades ago, he has responded to most of the biggest natural disasters of the last decade, both on behalf of the United Nations, Microsoft Disaster Response, NetHope, and the Icelandic government. Following the devastating earthquake in Haiti 2010, Gisli led the first international rescue team that arrived in the country.

The combination of Gisli's extensive field experience in disaster management and his technology background has led him to be appointed to various advisory boards and committees, such as the US State Department's sub-committee on the use of technology in international disasters.

Gisli currently serves as the Emergency Response Director of NetHope, a consortium of fortyone of the leading non-governmental organizations (NGOs) worldwide. A native of Iceland, he lives in the United States in Seattle, Wasington along with his wife, 5 teenage children and a Golden Labrador.

Acknowledgements

Never underestimate the power of a small group of people to change the world. In fact, it is the only way it ever has.

Margaret Mead

The idea behind this book had been in my mind for a long time, but it wasn't until November 2012 that I really challenged myself to get it done.

The method I used was to publicly go out there and tell the world that I was about to write a book. In addition to telling everyone I was about to write a book, I set up a KickStarter project to raise funds for the work by allowing people to effectively pre-order copies of the book.

This KickStarter project, which was launched in early December 2012 also served as a great motivation for me, because it showed me that people really wanted to hear what I had to say. A month after launching the project, a total of 184 people had supported the project! Without this support the book would never have become a reality. To all of you I owe you endlessly for supporting me and believing in my dream.

To all of you, many of who already are my friends and colleagues, I am forever grateful and say my thanks by putting all of your names here in my book:

Aðalsteinn Gunnar Jóhannsson, Aki Salo, Alex Comninos, Alois Hirschmugl, Anders Laukvik, Andreas Lehmann, Anna Hallenborg, Antoine Bertout, Antoine Carriere, Ari Daníelsson, Árni Þór Birgisson, Baldvin Jónsson, Bas Lijnse, Ben Baker, Bert Brugghemans, Bill Baker, Bjoern Hendel, Bjørn Bendix, Bragi Reynisson, Brandon Greenberg, Brent Mayabb, Brent Ozar, Brynja S. Blomsterberg, Caroline Milligan, Catherine Graham, Cathy Koop, Cédric Moro, Chad Hobson, Chris Weeks, Christian Gomez, Cindy

Forbes, Clair Deevy, Corey Arnez Griffin, Corina Torseth, Cristoph Dennemoser, Dagbjartur Kr. Brynjarsson, Dan Farella, Darrell O'Donnell, Dean Walton, Debra Jacobs, Demetrios Pyrros, Donald Farmer, Eduardo Jerzierski, Edward G. Happ, Edward Hancox, Eero Pykalainen, Einar Þorsteinsson, Eric Rasmussen, Esty Sutyoko, FoxFury Lighting Solutions, Frank M. Michelsen, Frank Schott, Frederick Spielberg, George Durham, George Mu'ammar, Gordie Meyer, Greg Kramer, Guðbrandur Örn Arnarson, Guðjón S. Guðjónsson, Guðmundur Harðarson, Guðmundur Óskarsson, Gunnar Hólmsteinn, H. Can Ünen, Halldór Björnsson, Hans Gufler, Heather Leson, Helga Waage, Helgi Bachmann, Herdís Sigurjónsdóttir, Hiro Murata, Hjálmar Gíslason, Hjörtur Smárason, Hugh Pyle, Inga Wilson, Jack Levy, Jack Pagotto, James Panek, Jan Harboe, Jason Carlson, Jelle Janssens, Jemilah Mahmood, Jesper Aaberg, Jesper Holmer Lund, Jessica Ports, Joanna Lane, Joanne Ho, Joe Simmons, Jóhanna Axelsdóttir, John Cawcutt, John McGrath, John Westerdahl, Jói Sigurðsson, Jonathan Kushner, Jordana Orange, Josef Reiterer, Júlíus Gunnarsson, Kate Krukiel, Kenny Meesters, Kim Fields, Kirk Klaas, Koji Nonshita, Leah Etienne, Lisa Obradovich, Lyann Bradbury, María Edwardsdóttir, Marianne Allison, Marie-Sophie Reck, Marla Nykyri, Matthew Walker, Nathan Richardsson, Nicolas Nguyen, Nihan Erdogan, Nikolas Kühn Hove, Oddur Snær Magnússon, Ólafur Andri Ragnarsson, Ólafur Jón Jónsson, Ólafur Rögnvaldsson, Örn Kristinsson, Paige Dearing, Pangiotis Alevantis, Paolo Palmero, Pascal Schuback, Patrick Svenburg, Paul Berquam, Paul Chiswell, Paul Hengeveld, Per Hallenborg, Peter Friis-Mikkelsen, Phoebe Wynn-Pope, Riccardo De Marchi Trevisan, Rob Munro, Robert E. Dunne, Robert Greenberg, Robert Kirkpatrick, Robert Spiegel, Robin Schofield, Rolf Bakken, Roo Carole Horn, Ryan Burch, Ryan Ho, Sam Johnson, Samuel Gyger, Sara Farmer, Sarah Rescoe, Scott Fox, Shadrock Roberts, Shaun Robinson, Shawn Carlson, Shoreh Elhami, Sigríður Guðmundsdóttir, Sigurður Óli Sigurðsson, Sigurður Orri Þórhannesson, Sigurður Viktor Úlfarsson, Sjaak Seen, Snorri Páll Haraldsson, Stefanía Stefánsdóttir, Steve Birnbaum, Steve Meyer, Stuart Adams, Susanne Jul, Sveinn Benediktsson, Sverrir Berg, Terry Hardy, TH Schee, Thanh Le, Theodora Pétursdóttir, Thomas Peter, Tina Lee, TK McConnell, Tómas Tómasson, Tony Surma, Torben Marcussen, Tóti Stefánsson, Víðir Reynisson, Viggó Viggósson, Vilhjálmur Halldórsson, Wei-Sen Li, Willow Brugh, Winston Chang, Yves D'Eer, Þórir Guðmundsson, and Þorvarður Tjörvi Ólafsson

I also want to thank all the great people who helped me with various parts of the production process for this book. The great reviews from Brandon Greenberg, Brent Ozar, Jack Pagotto, Joanna Lane, Michael Elmquist, and Mirja Peters really helped make this book much more relevant and readable. My two fantastic volunteer editors Kristin Milburn Smith and Susanne Jul not only helped me improve the English grammar, but also provided me with so many suggestions on improvements, that I can never thank you well enough!!!

This book would never have become a reality if it wasn't for all the great people, especially my colleagues in ICE-SAR and UNDAC that have taught me so much about crisis leadership. You are my inspiration and it is an honor to have through the years been able to work with you in various crisis situations.

I also want to especially thank two of my mentors throughout my crisis leadership journey, Jesper Holmer Lund and Jemilah Mahmood. From you I have come to understand leadership comes from the heart. From you I have learned the importance of placing the people we are there to help at the forefront of everything we do. You have believed in me and from you I have learned so much. Your friendship, encouragement, and endless teaching has made me a better crisis leader.

I also want to thank my son, Axel Örn Gíslason, for designing the cover of this book. For some reason he managed to developed artistic capabilities, even when his parents had none.

Finally I want to thank all of my family, who has stood with me through thick and thin. You always believe in what I do and stand behind me in everything I do. My wife Sonja, is the real hero in the family, because she is the one who keeps running the house, while I jump on the next plane to respond to the next disaster. Without your endless support and love – none of this would have been possible.

Preface

You can't give strength to someone unless you have it inside you.

Anthony Robbins

It was 10:25pm on a cold January evening in 2010 and I had just got into bed, ready to watch the Sunday evening television programs. I connected my mobile phone to the charger, conveniently located on my nightstand, a position it has been for the last 16 years ready to wake me up in the middle of the night to go respond to a person lost or in need of rescue. Little did I know I was about to go on my most important rescue mission ever, responding to the devastating earthquake in Haiti that killed over 300,000 people.

This journey started 17 years earlier, when I became a volunteer in one of Iceland's almost 100 rescue teams. At my first training event, we had to rappel down a 20-meter high cliff-face, something that did not come easy for me, since I am afraid of heights. My search and rescue (SAR) career could have ended that afternoon, but I put my trust in the instructors and their roping expertise and gently moved towards the edge of the cliff and put my weight on the rope. After what felt like hours, I finally started rappelling down the cliff and when I got to the bottom I ran back up to do it again. I had overcome my initial fear and felt the strength of the adrenaline rush you get when you overcome your fears.

Through my almost 20 years of doing search and rescue around the world, I gradually moved from running up the mountains looking for a missing person to directing the teams doing the hard legwork as an incident manager. I discovered that my ability to keep my head clear and organize things in the middle of a chaotic environment were the key strengths needed to manage complex incidents where lives were at stake.

My volunteer journey was my way of giving back to my community. It came as a surprise to many of my friends and colleagues from the technology industry that I had been working in since the age of 14. For the first 13 years of my volunteer career, these two passions in life, disasters, and technology were separate. In 2007, I was fortunate enough that my employer, Microsoft, actually wanted to pay me a salary for combining these two passions. I started to work as a trusted advisor to governments and international organizations on how to leverage technology to more effectively respond to disasters.

Two years earlier, my national disaster management experience had turned international when I joined a unique group of emergency managers from around the world called UNDAC, the United Nations Disaster Assessment and Coordination team, that the United Nations dispatches as the initial coordinators of the international response in major disasters. Around the same time, the Icelandic Association for Search and Rescue (ICE-SAR) approached me and asked me to become one of the team leaders of the Icelandic Urban Search and Rescue Team (Team ICE-SAR), which I agreed to.

That cold January evening, like all information addicts, I checked my email before going to sleep. With the arrival of smartphones, this had become even easier, and as I was plugging it into the charger, I read the newly arrived emails. One in particular caught my eye. It was from the National Oceanic and Atmospheric Administration (NOAA) and their tsunami warning system. As I read it, I became alarmed.

An earthquake measuring 7.0 on the Richter scale had occurred just off the coast of Haiti. My lack of geology showed, because the initial reaction of my mind was "Can the Caribbean have an earthquake." The second reaction was "Darn, if this is true, then this is really bad!"

Less than 23 hours later, I was again facing my fear of heights. I had to climb down a ladder out of a 757-200 plane from Icelandair that had brought the ICE-SAR Urban Search and Rescue team for the most demanding mission it had ever undertaken. It was my role to lead this exceptional team through the most chaotic environment anyone can expect to experience.

This book brings together lessons I have learned in leading teams in times of crisis. The backdrop of the book is the story of response to one of the most devastating natural disasters of the past 100 years. However, it is important to remember that the foundation to a successful response is the effort put into planning and preparing for when a crisis strikes. As we uncover the principles of leading in times of crisis, we will also look back at how we ensure those principles are in place well before the need arises to rely upon them.

You may not plan to lead a team through an extreme crisis like a natural disaster, but the principles explained and the lessons described in this book apply to any crisis, small or large, where you are called upon to lead yourself and your team or organization through difficult times.

Snoqualmie, Washington – December 2013
Gisli Rafn Olafsson

How to Read This Book

> If your actions inspire others to dream more, learn more, do more, and become more, you are a leader.
>
> **John Quincy Adams**

There are seven sections in this book each of which builds upon the material covered in the previous sections. Thus, the recommendation is to read it sequentially. Once you have read the whole book, it is my hope that you will find the material covered so useful that you will be glancing through sections that touch you specifically at various times for years to come as you enjoy your journey through leadership.

The first section covers what crisis and crisis leadership are and how they affect all of us. This provides a theoretical background to the subsequent sections.

The second and third section focus on preparing you to lead in a crisis. In section two, the focus is on becoming a crisis leader. It discusses what happens when you become a leader in an already existing team or organization. It also provides you with insights into how to tackle difficult situations arising from prior leadership in the organizations. The third section focuses on how you can make your team or organization more resilient to crises. Improving resilience is one of the best ways you can ensure that your role as a crisis leader becomes as easy as possible.

The fourth, fifth and sixth sessions all are about what happens during a crisis. The fourth section focuses on the initial chaotic period of a crisis. In it, you will learn about how the confusion and chaos affects you and how you might react. The fifth section then tackles the important subject of decision making in times of crisis. It looks at the importance of good information and different methods of decision making. In the sixth section, we will look at team dynamics during a crisis and tackles important subjects such as team morale and stress.

In the seventh and final section, we will talk about the time after the chaos subsides and the importance of follow up.

Finally, a note about the use of pronouns in the book. The pronoun "I" refers to me, the author. The pronoun "you" refers to you, the crisis leader.

Now, let us get started on our crisis leadership adventure.

SECTION 1

The Crisis Leader

Whatever you are, be a good one!

Abraham Lincoln

You never know when a crisis will strike and when it will become your turn to lead your organization, team, or community through the crisis. In this book, you will learn the key principles of leadership that you should keep in mind when a crisis hits. To start with, let us define crisis and crisis leadership.

A Crisis Leader: Chapter 1

Crisis, Chaos, Despair

True courage is being afraid, and going ahead and doing your job anyhow, that's what courage is.

General Norman Schwarzkopf

In this chapter I will start by defining what I mean by a crisis and then I will look at some of the characteristics of a crisis, such as the chaotic environment that follows the onset of a crisis and the despair that many feel when crisis strikes.

Defining Crisis

If we look for a dictionary[1] definition of a crisis then it provides us with the following:

1. A crucial or decisive point or situation; a turning point.

2. An unstable situation, in political, social, economic or military affairs, especially one involving an impending abrupt change.

3. A sudden change in the course of a disease, usually at which the patient is expected to recover or die.

4. (psychology) A traumatic or stressful change in a person's life.

1 Merriam-Webster online dictionary

5. (drama) A point in a drama at which a conflict reaches a peak before being resolved.

In their work, *What Is a Disaster? New Answers to Old Questions*, R.W. Perry and E.L. Quarantelli[2] emphasized that we don't consider a situation a crisis unless some aspects of human existence are affected negatively.

It is also important to note that in a crisis, change (often rapid change) is central to the definitions above.

A crisis is something that has a beginning, a crucial high point, and an end. A crisis can either be sudden-onset or have a protracted onset. An earthquake is an example of a sudden-onset crisis, while famines are examples of a protracted-onset crisis.

Sudden-onset crises and protracted-onset crises may at first seem different from one another, but most of the same leadership principles apply to both. The main difference is that a protracted-onset crisis can often be averted because you have time to respond before it reaches the crucial high point. Unfortunately, lack of leadership often results in the issues not being addressed until becomes a crisis.

In this book there is a strong focus on building resilience, "the ability to become strong, healthy, or successful again after something bad happens"[3]. This is because it is through resiliency and leadership at all levels in your organization that you can prevent crises from ever reaching the critical phase.

Before the Icelandic economy collapsed in October 2010, multiple academics, analysts, and staff within the banking system had raised warning flags. Poor leadership at all levels, however, meant that those flags were dismissed or ignored. When the dominos started falling, some of those who had been in leadership positions suffered nervous breakdowns or became catatonic because they realized that those flags had actually been true. At that point, the crisis had reached a critical phase where options to respond were very limited.

---

2 Perry, R.W. and Quarantelli, E.L. (2004): What Is a Disaster? New Answers to Old Questions, Xlibris Press, Philadelphia, PA.

3 Merriam-Webster on-line dictionary

The Six Human Needs

While each human being is unique, we also share nervous systems that function in the same way. There are also six fundamental needs that everyone has in common, and all behavior is simply an attempt to meet those six needs. This drive is encoded in our nervous system.

1. Certainty: assurance you can avoid pain and gain pleasure

2. Uncertainty/Variety: the need for the unknown, change, new stimuli

3. Significance: feeling unique, important, special or needed

4. Connection/Love: a strong feeling of closeness or union with someone or something

5. Growth: an expansion of capacity, capability or understanding

6. Contribution: a sense of service and focus on helping, giving to and supporting others

The means by which people meet these six human needs are unlimited. For example, one of the six human needs is the desire for certainty that we can avoid pain and gain pleasure (i.e. comfort). Some people pursue this need by striving to control all aspects of their lives, while others obtain certainty by giving up control and adopting a philosophy of faith.

Variety makes us feel alive and engaged. Then there's the desire for significance—a belief that one's life has meaning and importance. Some individuals will pursue this need by competing with others, or by destroying and tearing down those around them. Others may strive to fulfill this need through connection with other human beings.

The force of life is the drive for fulfillment; we all have a need to experience a life of meaning. Fulfillment can only be achieved through a pattern of living in which we focus on two spiritual needs: 1) the need to continuously grow; and 2) the need to contribute beyond ourselves in a meaningful way.

All dysfunctional behaviors arise from the inability to consistently meet these needs. When our attempts to reach fulfillment fail, we will settle for comfort—or for meeting our needs on a small scale. Look to replace any dis-empowering ways of meeting your needs with things that empower and support you and others.

Anthony Robbins
The 6 Human Needs – Why We Do What We Do

Chaos All Around

Chaos is the score upon which reality is written.

Henry Miller

Chaos is the key characteristic of a crisis. When crisis strikes, you experience chaos all around you. Many different emotions are rushing through your mind and that of everyone else involved. The situation in front of your eyes becomes surreal and sometimes you wonder if you are starring in a movie.

A crisis affects one of your key human needs (see sidebar – The Six Human Needs); the need for certainty and comfort. We all desire comfort. Much of this comfort comes from certainty. Of course, there is no absolute certainty, but we want the car to start, the water to flow from the tap, and the currency we use to hold its value.

How we deal with disruptions to this basic human need varies greatly. It affects some people so badly that they become catatonic, don't make decisions, don't move, and don't see a way out. At the other end of the spectrum you have people that keep calm, do not panic and start finding ways to bring things back to normal, understanding that the process may take a long time. These people understand that crisis is not a sprint. Crisis is a marathon.

It is important for you to look clearly at how disruptions to certainty and comfort affect you, and get a better understanding of your personal motivations behind that behavior. Often we compensate for the lack of certainty and comfort by focusing on other needs, such as the desire to contribute something of value, to help others, and to make the world a better place.

Levels of Crisis

> Wherever there is danger, there lurks opportunity;
> whenever there is opportunity, there lurks danger.
>
> **Earl Nightingale**

There are multiple levels of severity that a crisis can have and the way you behave during those different levels of severity often changes. It is important for you to understand how the different levels can affect you and others around you.

In his research[4], Professor Emeritus Dennis Mileti of University of Colorado at Boulder looks at levels of crisis in the context of natural disasters, and many of the same issues are apparent in other types of crises.

4 Mileti, Dennis S., Disasters by Design, National Academy of Sciences, Washington D.C., 1999

Mileti defines three levels of crisis: everyday emergencies (for example car accidents and house fires), disasters (for example earthquakes and floods), and catastrophes (for example Hiroshima). In the non-disaster world, we might consider these everyday crisis, major crises, and catastrophes.

According to Mileti, people are usually the cause of *everyday emergencies*, since they often do things they should not do. In these cases, he found that we look towards organizations to help us bring things back to normal. When people from these organizations (for example a firefighter or police officer) come to our assistance, we do not personalize their assistance, but rather refer to them by their profession.

In a *major crisis*, in contrast, organizations often become the problem, while people, often the employees of those organizations, end up being the ones solving the crisis. During a major crisis, organizations tend to fight for attention from the media and the public, fight political turf battles, and try to utilize the crisis to prove their importance and existence.

A great example of this can be found in almost any country in the world where you can ask a police department if they like their fire department or vice versa. Interestingly, even though they may seem united in the face of the major crisis—collaborating in the field, their leaders are often fighting massive turf battles with each other. The same also holds true in the international arena where the large UN agencies and the big NGOs often fight endless turf battles while people are suffering.

Luckily, as Mileti pointed out in his research, people often come to the rescue. It is through individuals ,in these organizations that collaboration happens, often against the political will of the organization. The reason, according to Mileti, is that those people feel a common bond towards doing "the right thing," leveraging two of the six basic human needs, the need for connection, and the need for contribution.

This individual collaboration is something I have witnessed numerous times, and most of the time it is not those with leadership titles that show this important aspect of crisis leadership. Usually it happens at the operational level, where people are experiencing the effects of the crisis first hand.

The final level of crisis, as defined by Mileti, is *catastrophes*. As examples of this he pointed at events like the dropping of the atomic bomb on Hiroshima, where a team of nurses came in, and as the number of people in serious condition doubled as every five minutes passed, they gave up, feeling totally overwhelmed by the situation.

Thankfully, Mileti pointed out two things that are positive about catastrophes. One is that they happen very seldom, and the other is that we usually snap out of this state of helplessness very quickly.

Mileti's research showed two more interesting findings. First, passing from one level of a crisis to another is not triggered by someone declaring the crisis to have reached another level, but by the observed change in behavior of the people involved. In other words, our behavior defines the level of the crisis, not a formal declaration of the level.

Second, when he surveyed all the emergency managers in the USA and asked them about how they could achieve better collaboration, only 30% of them understood that it was through people and not organizations that it happens. For crisis leaders it is therefore important to understand that when dealing with the chaos of a major crisis, they must work through people, not organizations.

Despair

At times like this the game goes to the one with the loudest voice, but everyone wishes their mother was there.

Captain Jack Harkness - Torchwood

During a crisis, it is often easy to simply give up and let despair take over. It is crucial for us to remember that as bad as things may seem at the height of the crisis, given enough time, things will become better. Giving up is always the easy way out: It takes the least amount of effort.

If you have been directly affected by the crisis you may experience this feeling of despair. But even if you have not been directly affected, it is important for you to understand its effect on those who were affected.

In times of despair, your focus is on the loss and how bad things are all around you. You cannot see any light at the end of the tunnel, because your focus is on the darkness. At such times, it is important for us to remember that all human emotions, including despair, are a result of feelings or a state of mind where your conscious focus generated a certain mental state.

All of our emotions are a result of our brain trying to achieve certainty—reduce pain and gain pleasure. The emotion of despair frees you from having to deal with the pain around you. The only way out of despair is to focus on things that allow you to gain pleasure that overrides the pain you feel.

As mentioned earlier, one of the best ways to achieve this is to focus on the basic human need of contribution. Your way out of despair is to contribute and help those around you. It is in times of crisis that heroes are born. Heroes are simply people who converted their pain into pleasure by contributing to others around them that were also affected by the crisis.

That brings us to the concept of crisis leadership…

Further reading

- Seven Lessons for Leading in Crisis by Bill George
- The Power of Positive Thinking by Norman Vincent Peale

A Crisis Leader: Chapter 2

Leadership

> You can't relate to a superhero, to a superman, but you can identify with a real man who in times of crisis draws forth some extraordinary quality from within himself and triumphs but only after a struggle.
>
> **Timothy Dalton**

Looking out for a Leader

> Walkin' among our people
> There's someone who's straight and strong
> To lead us from desolation
> And a broken world gone wrong
>
> **Neil Young – Looking for a Leader**

It is in times of crisis that leadership is most needed. It is also in these times that leaders without titles are born. It is in these times that those affected by chaos, confusion, and despair look towards others to tell them what they should be doing.

If you are the one with a leadership title then people look toward you, but the truth is that many in position of leadership are not ready to assume that responsibility in a crisis.

It is in the times of crisis that true leaders appear. Those leaders often rise way above their formal title or location in the organizational chart. The most junior member of the team may be the one to overcome the despair and have the ability to focus on resolving the challenges in front of them.

There are numerous examples of this throughout history. During the financial crisis in Iceland, it was not the governmental ministers or heads of the central bank that led the discussions with the international community to assist the country out of the challenges, but a junior economist within the central bank.

When a deadly earthquake struck Padang, Indonesia in the fall of 2009, crucial aspects of the international response were coordinated by two junior humanitarian workers, as we will learn more about in chapter 11.

What is Leadership?

Leadership should be born out of the understanding of the needs of those who would be affected by it.

Marian Anderson

This is a good time to define what I mean by leadership. We could go with the Merriam-Webster dictionary definition:

1. the capacity of someone to lead
2. a group of leaders
3. (dated) The office or status of a leader.

However, it simply leads us to the definition of a leader, which Merriam-Webster defines as:

1. Any person or thing that leads or conducts.
2. One who goes first.
3. One having authority to direct.

4. One who leads a political party or group of elected party members; sometimes used in titles.

5. A person or thing that leads in a certain field in terms of excellence, success, etc.

We must also distinguish between leadership and management as in the following quote from the management and leadership guru Peter Drucker: *"Management is doing things right; leadership is doing the right things".*

Leadership is about getting people to do the things you want them to do, without necessarily having the authority to tell them to do these things. Leadership is about sharing a vision of a future state and influencing others to help you reach that state. Leadership is about focusing on that future vision instead of the past, while leveraging the lessons of the past to ensure you do not make the same mistakes while trying to reach that future vision.

Influence vs. Authority

Leadership is about influence, not about authority.

Mohana Janam

Most organizations of the industrial age were built around the concepts of centralized authority and hierarchical organizational charts. They were based on the assumptions that individuals were performing small well-defined manual tasks and did not have the ability or need to see the big picture. As a result, management layers were introduced and each manager was responsible for overseeing the big picture of the people that reported to him or her. As the organization grew in size, managers of managers were needed to oversee the big picture of multiple groups and/or departments.

The challenge with this approach is that as the work became more complex and interconnected, the need arose for individuals to become more than just manual workers. In order to solve the complex issues they now faced, they had to find innovative solutions that required people from multiple departments to work together.

This is especially true when a crisis hits and the only way out is innovative out-of-the-box thinking. It is at these times that the organizational management hierarchy does not work, especially if those who normally lead became victims of their basic human need of certainty.

Over the past two decades, leadership gurus have recognized that influence is actually a much more important factor than authority. Your ability to influence people will get you much further than your authority over those people. Influence is all about getting others to share your vision of the future state rather than pushing them towards that future state. Those you manage to influence to share your vision will not only go towards that future by themselves, in many cases they will help you bring that vision to others.

Your Ability to Influence

> This new kind of business hero…must learn to operate without the might of the hierarchy behind them. The crutch of authority must be thrown away and replaced by their own ability to make relationships, use influence, and work with others to achieve results.
>
> **Rosabeth Moss Kanter**

As this powerful quote points out, your ability to influence others depends on a number of factors, such as networking, persuasion, and collaboration. In this and the next couple of chapters we will look at these factors and help you develop them.

While authority is something you be given based on your position in the corporate ladder, influence is something you can develop and earn regardless of your position on that ladder. The great byproduct of developing your ability to influence is that it is recognized by those above you, and in most cases will help you climb that corporate ladder.

Developing your ability to influence will touch not just your career, but also other aspects of your life. Just remember as you develop that ability to influence to use it for good. We'll cover more on that in a subsequent chapter.

Build a Rapport with Others

One of the key factors in your ability to influence others relies on your ability to build a rapport with other people. Master this ability and your connections to people will quickly move from establishing rapport to a relationship built on trust.

What is it that makes people want to build a rapport with you? The key is to make people feel you really care about what they are telling you, and that you really care about them and what they have to offer. Building a rapport with someone takes effort on both sides. The good thing is that when people feel that someone is genuinely interested in what they are saying or have to offer then they usually very rapidly want to establish that connection with you.

There is an old saying that points out that we have two ears, but only one mouth, hence we should listen more than we talk. The problem is that between those two ears we have trillions of brain cells that start processing what we hear and immediately want to respond.

A simple method for improving your ability to build a rapport with other people is to give your brain a break. There is no need to respond immediately while the other person is still talking to you. Genuinely listening to someone is a trait that true leaders have learned to develop. *Genuinely listening* means that you really listen to what the other person has to offer and don't interrupt with your views or stories.

We have all had experiences where we meet people for the first time and we immediately build that rapport with them. This often happens with people who share our views of the world and people whom we feel we can learn as much from as we can teach. If you analyze your interaction with these people you will quickly discover that you most likely spend as much time listening to what they have to say as you do talking to them.

Over the next few days and weeks, exercise your ability to genuinely listen. See the difference it will make in your ability to build a rapport with others.

Telling a Story

Better than a thousand hollow words is one word that brings peace.

Buddha

Many leaders fail to get people to follow them because of their inability to express their vision in a way that gets others excited about it. One of the key factors to developing influence is to develop the ability to express your vision. One of the best ways to express a vision is through storytelling.

The art of storytelling is as old as human speech. Stories have provided the foundation for many teaching traditions to pass down wisdom through the ages. Well-told stories help us develop a vision in our mind of the story being told. The better the storyteller, the clearer the vision becomes in our mind.

Stories are therefore a powerful tool in getting people to share your vision of the future. Remember that all human activities focus on avoiding pain and achieving pleasure. Stories have the power to raise both emotions in our minds.

If we tell powerful enough stories of the current state that focus on the pain that it causes, then those listening to your story will feel that pain, even though they are not experiencing it firsthand. At the same time when you start telling stories that paint a more pleasurable future vision, then those listening to your story will also feel that pleasure. Your ability to influence them therefore relies on your ability to make them feel that pain and pleasure alternate through your storytelling.

This is no newfound principle. Most religious writing, some of which is thousands of years old, relies on this approach to get people to follow their vision of what is right and wrong. In recent times, political spin-doctors have become experts at changing public opinion through storytelling that leverages this pain-pleasure principle.

What is important for you to realize is that your ability to express your vision to others relies on your ability to leverage those pain-pleasure principles in the way you tell the story of your vision. You must exercise your storytelling skills, just like an entrepreneur exercises their skills in pitching to the venture capitalist until they have it down to the 30-second elevator pitch.

When crisis strikes, those that can quickly develop a compelling vision of a compelling and believable future state where the crisis has been addressed, and have the ability to easily share that vision with others, will be the ones that rise up as crisis leaders.

The Speed of Trust

There is one thing that is common to every individual, relationship, team, family, organization, nation, economy and civilization throughout the world – one thing which if removed, will destroy the most powerful government, the most successful business, the most thriving economy, the most influential leadership, the greatest friendship, the strongest character, the deepest love. On the other hand if developed and leveraged, that one thing has the potential to create unparalleled success and prosperity in life. Yet, it is the least understood, most neglected, and most underestimated possibility of our time. That one thing is trust.

Stephen M. R. Covey

In his groundbreaking book, The Speed of Trust, Stephen M.R. Covey, son of acclaimed author and leadership guru Stephen R. Covey looks at the importance of trust in our lives. What makes trust different from many other traits is that it usually takes a long time to develop but can be lost in a matter of seconds.

Figure 1 - Waves of trust - Image courtesy of Franklin Covey™ - http://www.my-speedoftrust.com/

Covey pointed out that trust comes in a number of waves. The first one is self-trust, followed by relationship trust. Once we achieve those two, we can start focusing on stakeholder trust, which breaks down into organizational trust, market trust, and societal trust. Let us look at the first two, since they focus on the individual rather than the organization for which the individual works.

Self-trust is based on the principle of credibility. Credibility is built upon four core values:

- Integrity – Are your actions congruent with your values?
- Intent – Do you have hidden agendas?
- Capabilities – Are you relevant?
- Results – What is your track record?

Before you can start building relationship trust, you must focus on building your own credibility. Relationship trust is strongly based on how you get out of problems you have gotten yourself into. Covey identified thirteen key behaviors that influenced how others trust you in a relationship:

1. Talk straight

2. Demonstrate respect
3. Create transparency
4. Right wrongs
5. Show loyalty
6. Deliver results
7. Get better
8. Confront reality
9. Clarify expectations
10. Practice accountability
11. Listen first
12. Keep commitments
13. Extend trust

These key behaviors are especially important in times of crisis. It is during these times that you need to build relationship trust quickly to gain followers and achieve your vision of a future state. We will be touching on a number of these behaviors in later chapters of the book.

It is when you violate any of these cores or behaviors that you will lose the trust of others. Depending on the severity of the violation that trust can be lost in a matter of seconds, or over a period of time. When that happens, it is essential for you to quickly identify which principles you have violated and start working on restoring trust in your abilities to address them. Remember the first behavior of talking straight and admitting your failures quickly. Cover-up and denial of error erode trust most rapidly.

Further reading

- How to Win Friends and Influence People by Dale Carnegie
- Speed of Trust by Stephen M.R. Covey

A Crisis Leader: Chapter 3

Characteristics of a Successful Crisis Leader

Life begins at the end of your comfort zone.

Neale Donald Walsch

What Makes a Good Crisis Leader?

A question I often get asked is, "What makes a good crisis leader?" "What is it in their character that makes them better prepared to become a leader in times of crisis?" In this chapter, we will look at some of the characteristics of good leaders, which in my experience are essential in making someone better prepared and better positioned to lead during a time of crisis.

Humility

I hate being idolized. When People try to think too highly of you, you fall in love with yourself. I lose my sense of who I am and what I want to do.

Dr. Jemilah Mahmood

Humility is all about knowing yourself as you truly are, not as an idealized version of yourself. In today's competitive society it is often hard to remember this. As you rise through the corporate ladder, or as your great work gets media coverage, it is easy to get lost in the glamour of the fancy titles of your job, or by the mentions of the media.

Those who show leadership in times of crisis often are idolized as heroes. For many people this stamp imprints on their forehead and they live in the glamour for their 15 minutes of fame. Sadly, there are countless stories about those who try to live in that limelight for the rest of their lives, not realizing that true leadership takes more than just one victory.

True crisis leaders understand their own shortcomings and keep the focus on achieving the greater good, rather than their own short-lived success. True crisis leaders set aside the power and authority that comes with their title and are willing to serve those that work for them. True crisis leaders make themselves accountable to those that report to them, knowing that those are the people who give them power.

Humility is also about knowing that no matter what you do in a crisis, you will never be able to help everyone. What really matters is doing the best you can do. I frequently use the story of the starfish and the woman on the beach to give people a good understanding of why every action contributes to the overall puzzle:

> [illegible]
> [illegible]
> *figure in the distance moving like a dancer. As he*
> [illegible]
> [illegible]
> *to the sand, picking up a starfish and very gently*
> [illegible]
>
> [illegible]
> *starfish into the ocean?"*
>
> [illegible]
> [illegible]

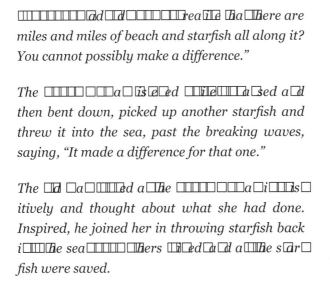

□□□□□□□□ad□d□□□□□□rea□i□e □ha□□here are miles and miles of beach and starfish all along it? You cannot possibly make a difference."

The □□□□□□□□a□is□e□ed □□i□e□□□a□sed a□d then bent down, picked up another starfish and threw it into the sea, past the breaking waves, saying, "It made a difference for that one."

The □□d □a□□□□□ed a□□he □□□□□□□□a□i□□□is□ itively and thought about what she had done. Inspired, he joined her in throwing starfish back i□□□he sea□□□□□□hers □□i□ed□a□d a□□he s□ar□ fish were saved.

Loren Eiseley, recreated by the Starfish Charity

True crisis leaders know that they are only a small piece of a grand puzzle, but by providing leadership, they are able to get others to become part of that grand puzzle and address the problems at hand. Each of those pieces vary. Some roles are more visible and prominent than others, but without someone addressing the difficult, non-visible roles, the overall effort would falter. True crisis leaders acknowledge this and help everyone to realize this important concept.

Courage

What holds us back in life is the invisible architecture of our fear.

Robin Sharma

True crisis leaders are willing to step outside of their normal comfort zone and embrace their fear of the unknown instead of allowing it to paralyze them. True crisis leaders are willing to jump into the unknown and take on any challenges they may face consequently. True crisis leaders are willing to find innovative new solutions to the current challenges instead of always relying on the solutions of the past.

Courage is not about jumping out of a plane wearing a parachute. Courage is about facing your everyday fears. Courage is about getting rid of the shackles that stop you from being the best you can be.

As I mentioned in the preface, my first experience as a rescue volunteer trainee was to rappel of a cliff. For someone who has a fear of heights, that might have been the end of my career as a search and rescue volunteer. But because I decided to face my fear, I overcame this small hindrance, and started rather than ended my career.

Knowing that I could easily overcome that fear of heights certainly proved useful when I had to climb down a ladder out of the Boeing 757-300 that brought us to Haiti in January 2010. It would not have been a pretty sight if my colleagues had to carry me down that ladder.

Fear like any other emotion, is the brain's way of trying to associate pain with a particular future situation. Just like we can overcome other emotions by finding things of pleasure that are stronger than the anticipated pain, we can overcome our fears by focusing on positive emotions that are stronger.

Growing up, I developed this fear of seeing people who had died. I do not know if it was related to losing my father and grandfather at an early age or if it came from my fear of ghosts and the dark, but it was something that stuck with me for a very long time.

Then, in 2001, tragedy struck our family again when my stepfather was diagnosed with terminal cancer. Instead of spending the last weeks of his life in a hospital, he stayed at home. I had just moved back to Iceland from the USA and was living in the house along with my two sons. As his last moments came, I was there, along with my mother and a doctor who was an old friend of my stepfather.

Witnessing someone die was much more peaceful than I had anticipated, and after he passed away, I helped the doctor prepare his body. For me the ability to be there to support my mother provided me with more "pleasure" than the "pain" of my fear of seeing a dead person.

Little did I know that this personal experience would nine years later help me tremendously in dealing with the sights that awaited us as we landed in Port-au-Prince, Haiti. It is hard to imagine what my psychological reaction would have been if I had not overcome my fear of seeing dead people, because those first days in Haiti, we saw tens of thousands of bodies on the streets and hundreds of bodies in collapsed buildings in which we searched for survivors.

Conviction

They thought that the bullets would silence us, but they failed. And out of that silence came thousands of voices.

Malala Yousafzai

True crisis leaders follow their passion and conviction even when things are tough. True crisis leaders do not change course simply because they faces adversity.

Conviction is not about resisting change. Conviction is about never giving up no matter how hard things get. Conviction is about believing in yourself and your ability to overcome challenges that come your way.

When dealing with a crisis it is often tempting to give up or do "the easy thing." The obvious solution is often the wrong one, and it is usually the tough things that need to be done. It is accomplishing those tough things that help build your character, and make you more resilient in dealing with future adversity.

When taking over as team leader for ICE-SAR's USAR team, I was convinced that it could become one of the best urban search and rescue teams in the world. Leveraging the passion of volunteers to achieve lofty goals is something I deeply believe in. When I took over, the team had its share of history. There were a number of challenges that had to be overcome, most prominently building a cohesive and unified team that functioned well together. I knew that the team had the skills to perform the search and rescue portion of the effort. But I also knew that it would take a lot of work to make the team ready for the overall task of responding to a major earthquake.

Over the coming years I faced many challenges, and at times it would have been much easier for me to simply walk away and focus on other aspects of my disaster response career. But, by consistently refusing to give up, and continually pushing for things to improve, we were able to turn ourselves into a well functioning team.

As a crisis leader you need to keep your conviction and be patient. Things may not happen at the speed you want them to happen, but if you have prepared your team properly, things will get done.

Authenticity

The privilege of a lifetime is to become who you truly are.

C.G. Jung

True crisis leaders not only "talk the talk" but "walk the walk." True crisis leaders do not tell their team to do one thing, and then do the opposite thing themself. True crisis leaders are true to their word and only commit to things they have faith they can achieve.

Authenticity is all about being true to what you stand for. Authenticity is about letting your actions speak for you, instead of simply talking about things. Authenticity is about being true to your own character.

True crisis leaders are not afraid to get their hands dirty and join their team in doing the difficult tasks. A good way for a crisis leader to demonstrate their authenticity is by having an open leadership style. Through talking about the situation and issues at hand openly, the crisis leaders demonstrate that they are not hiding anything from their team. By asking the team to help address the situation, they encourage the team. Through listening to their feedback and suggestions, the crisis leaders can show in an authentic manner that they believe in the capacity of their team.

Kindness

> Kindness is a language which the deaf can hear and the blind can see.
>
> **Mark Twain**

True crisis leaders show compassion for those affected by the crisis. True crisis leaders fight to resolve the crisis to improve the situation for those affected. True crisis leaders lead with their heart.

Leveraging the passion of kindness is one of the best ways to motivate yourself in dealing with the difficulties ahead. When matters go beyond your own ambitions, the reward for doing the difficult task is so much higher.

I have often been asked why I leave my family behind in the middle of the night, or leave a Christmas dinner to go search for missing people. People ponder what it is that gets me to spend more time of my search and rescue volunteer work than on my paying day job. My answer to them is simple. It is the smile of a face of a parent reunited with a missing child, or the joy expressed by a family when they receive news that their loved ones have been located. These smiles and this joy are like an injection that fills my heart with a passion required to respond at a moment's notice at any time of the day.

The reward of expressing kindness toward others is one of the most powerful drugs on the planet. You can leverage it to motivate yourself to overcome any challenges and difficulties that you face. Furthermore, it is this power that enables you to drive forward change in this world much faster than any other means.

Further reading

- Give and Take by Adam Grant
- Inside the Leader's Mind by Liz Mellon
- The 7 Habits of Highly Successful People by Steven R. Covey
- The Speed of Trust by Stephen M. R. Covey

A Crisis Leader: Chapter 4

The Development of Character and Values

I learnt that courage was not the absence of fear, but the triumph over it.

Nelson Mandela

Defining Character and Value

Before we start discussing the importance of character and values it is good to define what we mean by these terms.

Character is one of the attributes or features that make up and distinguish an individual. It describes the complex of mental and ethical traits marking, and often individualizing, a person.

In ethics, *value* denotes the significance we attach to something with the aim of determining what the best action to take is, or life to live.

In times of crisis both of these aspects become very important. If crisis leaders lack a strong character or strong values, they are bound to fail when facing adversity.

Building a strong character

Nearly all men can stand adversity, but if you want to test a man's character, give him power.

Abraham Lincoln

Your character develops throughout your life. It reflects the lessons learned from your experiences in life. It is, however, possible for you to increase the strength of your character through a number of ways. You can read books that help you develop your understanding of yourself and the world around you. You can seek out experiences that help you develop your character. You can set personal goals that allow you to grow as a human being. Let us look at these different ways in more detail.

You can focus on understanding yourself better. You should try to get clear definitions of the moral qualities you want to construct for yourself. Break down each definition into parts that you easily understand. Use your own words to define these qualities. Think of practical applications for those qualities. When might you need this particular quality or trait? Are there ways for you to exercise it? What might you experience when you exercise it? Leverage books, websites and other material for your research.

When you have gained a better understanding of the qualities you want to achieve, you need to develop a strong longing for them. Just like you develop a desire for a nice fast car, you need to create a huge passion for achieving these qualities. Think about how this quality will improve your life. Think about how it will make you feel. Think about how your family and friends will perceive you following this transformation. It is not enough for you to understand compassion or kindness. You must long to be compassionate and kind. These visualization exercises allow you to perform mental rehearsals of desired patterns of thinking and behaving.

Once you have built these desires, you must set goals. Desire by itself is not enough. You should set yourself goals with due dates and milestones. These milestones should help you track your journey towards building a strong character by exposing measurable results towards these goals. Make sure you don't just track the final endpoints, also track intermediate transformational points, or milestones, along the way.

Finally, you must take action. Lofty desires and grand plans don't result in change. Specific daily actions do. You must make conscious, daily efforts to bring those qualities into your life. You must maintain never ending passion in action. Force yourself to take those daily small steps and you will reap the benefits.

Understanding your own value system

By having an understanding of your own values you will gain tremendous clarity and focus. This clarity can then be used to make consistent decisions and take committed action. In other words, the whole point of discovering your own values is to improve the results you get in those areas that are truly most important to you.

You will be able to leverage this clarity of your values to help guide you through the difficult times of a crisis. They help you prioritize things in the midst of the chaos.

There are two main reasons this is important to us. The first reason we need to be able to leverage and lean upon our values is that time is our most limited resource. This is particularly true during a crisis such as natural disasters, where wasting time can result in lives being lost. If we waste our time by investing it in actions that don't produce the results we want, that loss is permanent.

The second reason we need to be able to use our values is that we human beings tend to be fairly inconsistent in how we invest our time and energy. Most of us are easily distracted by things going on around us. Nowhere is that more evident as it is in the chaotic environment of a crisis. It's easy for us to fall into the trap of following different priorities every day. If we don't consciously use our values to stick to clear and consistent priorities, we'll naturally drift off course and shift all over the place. In the worst case scenarios, this can make the difference between life and death for those we are working to assist and the consequent loss of leadership.

Be aware of these two reasons - limited time and our typically high distractibility – to help you focus on consciously knowing and living by your values. Our values act as our compass to put us back on course every single day. They help us stay on the course that takes us closer and closer to our own definition of the "best" outcome we could possibly experience.

You also need to take into consideration the organizational values of the entity you work for. How do the organizational values match your own values? If they are well aligned you are most likely in a fulfilling job. If they are not aligned, perhaps you should look for new place to work.

Further reading

- It's Your Ship by Michael Abrashoff
- It's Our Ship by Michael Abrashoff
- Barefoot Leadership by Alvin Ung
- The Alchemist by Paulo Coelho
- The Monk Who Sold his Ferrari by Robin Sharma
- The Secret Letters from the Monk Who Sold His Ferrari by Robin Sharma

A Crisis Leader: Chapter 5

Preparing Yourself for Crisis

By failing to prepare, you are preparing to fail.

Benjamin Franklin

Always Expect a Crisis

If crisis always came at a predefined day and in a predefined form, then preparing for it would be easy. You would have the other 364 days of the year to get yourself ready for it. However, the very nature of a crisis is that it can occur at any time, and somehow it always happens when you least expect it.

Little did I know that cold January day in 2010 that a few hours later all my plans for that month, and actually the next few months would be turned upside down. I was in the process of planning a trip to the Philippines, followed by a visit to Seattle, in what would have been my first "around the world" trip.

Yet when the crisis hit, my mind did not panic, but went into a process-oriented mode. It went down all the processes that we had put in place and exercised for exactly this type of crisis. I knew whom to contact, what questions would be asked, and what had to be done before we could even consider taking off for a faraway country.

The Role of Preparedness

There's no harm in hoping for the best as long as you're prepared for the worst.

Stephen King

Preparedness is one of the keys to staying calm when a crisis hits. By having thought through the different processes that you need to deal with during different types of crises, it will help you even though the crisis that you experience is not the same as the one that for which you prepared.

Being a true crisis leader means that you do not focus exclusively on the response part. This is sometimes the most "sexy" part. It is in this part that you get to be in the limelight and shine. But if you do not put focus on preparing for the response, then you will end up with the spotlight on you while you do not know how to respond. This is because your brain never went through the process of preparing for the crisis.

The World Bank asked world-renowned economists to look at the importance of preparedness in the disaster response field[5]. Their findings were amazing. They discovered that for every dollar spent on preparedness, six dollars are saved in the response. Although their study focused on disaster response, it can be estimated that the same factor applies for the relationship to any kind of crisis preparedness and crisis response.

In this chapter, we will talk about the role of personal preparedness. We will focus on preparedness of teams and organizations in Section 3.

How Will You React?

Every reaction is an opportunity to cultivate a pearl - a beautiful truth that will illuminate the way forwards.

Pollyanna Darling

5 Natural Hazards, Unnatural Disasters - https://www.gfdrr.org/nhud-home

Think back to any time in your past that you have had to deal with a crisis. How did you react? What emotions went through your mind as you discovered that the crisis had hit? What emotions went through your mind as you dealt with the crisis? What emotions went through your mind as the crisis ended?

Understanding and analyzing your own emotional response to crisis gives you an insight into how you might react to similar crisis in the future. What if the situation was twice as bad as what you have already experienced? What if the situation is ten times as bad? What if it affects you directly? What would your emotions then be?

Our mind is an amazing tool because we can actually imagine different scenarios like this and predict what our emotional response might be. We can also look back at experiences we have gone through and analyze why we reacted the way we did.

The human mind is also remarkable in the way that it does not just directly provide a reaction to external stimuli. Our brain and our thought process can actually control our emotional reaction to outside stimuli.

As mentioned earlier most of our actions are focused on two goals - reducing pain and increasing pleasure. Psychologists and self-improvement gurus understand this concept and leverage it to help people overcome difficult behaviors and fears.

As you analyze each emotional reaction you experience due to outside crisis stimuli, think about how that reaction was an attempt to reduce pain and increase pleasure. Determine what pain you were trying to address, and then look at whether the emotional reaction was helpful or not in dealing with the issue at hand. If it was helpful, then reinforce that behavior by accepting it as a way to decrease pain and increase pleasure.

If, on the other hand, your reaction was not helpful in dealing with the situation, then determine what action would have been more helpful. Identify ways in which you can make your mind associate less pain and increased pleasure with this better reaction. Then, go through that scenario repeatedly in your mind until it feels natural to you.

This simple method can be very helpful in getting your mind to be better prepared for dealing with crises in the future. The key is to use this method of mental rehearsal of the desired rather than undesired behavior to learn from your failures in the past, enforce the successes, and not to use it to dwell on the failures and beat yourself up for having made those mistakes. Remember that mistakes are only mistakes if you do not learn from them and continue to repeat them.

Self-Awareness

The act of discovering who we are will force us to accept that we can go further than we think.

Paulo Coelho

One of the best ways to prepare yourself for dealing with a crisis is to develop your own self-awareness. The more you understand yourself the better you will be at predicting how you will deal with what the crisis throws at you. The more you understand your own mental and physical state, the better you know how much you can take. The more aware you are of your own limitations and the more self-confident you are in admitting them, the better prepared are you to deal with the chaotic environment of the times ahead.

There is an old saying that in order to love others you first need to know how to love yourself. The same holds true for helping others. In order to be able to help others in times of crisis, you first need to be able to help yourself deal with it.

Physical State

Health is a state of complete physical, mental and social well-being, and not merely the absence of disease or infirmity.

Constitution of the World Health Organization

One of the things I learned the hard way was that in order to cope with a crisis, you need to be in a good physical state before the crisis happens. I am not talking about being in top athletic form but that your body is in good enough condition to take the prolonged stress that you will put on it during the crisis response period.

It is a well-known fact that stress does not just cause your mind to suffer. It is a whole-body experience. It is interesting to see old injuries reappear during a crisis response, because your body has not really fully recovered. Many leaders dramatically fail in their crisis response because their body simply cannot take the stress.

Make sure you keep your physical state in good condition at all times. Make sure you exercise regularly, and aim for exercises that build endurance as opposed to speed, because crisis response is a multi-day marathon, not a 100-meter sprint. Make sure you are getting regular sleep, because having to start crisis response in a state of sleep-deprivation is always bad.

If you have gone through some medical issues in the past, discuss with your doctor beforehand what signs you should look out for when you have to go through periods of stress. Many times, they will give you a great insight into what to do in order to prepare yourself for that marathon.

Prepare Your Family

Behind every great person is even a greater spouse
that keeps the wheels rolling in times of crisis.

Gisli Olafsson

One aspect that often is forgotten is the importance of preparing the family for times of crisis. When I joined a search and rescue (SAR) team in Seattle in the late 1990's, one of the first things that they discussed was that you first had to make your home and family disaster ready before you could go respond to a disaster.

There is a very important reason they put focus on this particular preparedness. If your mind is constantly worrying about what the situation may be back home, then you will not be able to put focus on responding to the crisis.

Tell your friends, spouse and your children that someday you may need to deal with a crisis, and that when you do, you will need their full support in ensuring you can put your focus on the crisis. You must also think about what assuming the role of crisis leader may have on your professional life. If you are a CEO who has to focus on a crisis within your company, then you better have someone ready to take on leadership in other areas.

I have always said that the real hero in my family is my wife. Through the years, she has always kept things running when I jump out the door with a moment's notice to deal with yet another crisis. Without her taking on the extra load in times of crisis to keep our family of five kids running I would never have been able to do the work I have done. To have a spouse who is willing to be the single parent, with one extra child (you) that is away on a field trip, is priceless.

Having those discussions and making possible arrangements for dealing with future crises are very important steps in preparing yourself for being able to respond to the next crisis at a moment's notice.

Further reading

- Mind Power Into the 21st Century by John Kehoe
- The Unthinkable by Amanda Ripley
- Ready.GOV

SECTION 2

Becoming a Leader

Begin at the beginning and go on till you come to the end; then stop.

Lewis Carroll

We have all been in the position of starting a new job or taking on a new role. In some cases, you come to a brand new environment where nobody knows you. In other cases, you take on a new role in an environment where people know you, but they may not be sure you are the right person for the role.

The latter was the case when I started as a new leader in the ICE-SAR team. I had worked alongside many of the team members in various missing people searches or rescues in the past, but urban search and rescue (USAR) was not an area I had worked in previously.

The ICE-SAR urban search and rescue team was formed in 1999 following a devastating earthquake that hit Izmir, Turkey. The ICE-SAR team deployed again to earthquakes in Algiers in 2003 and Morocco in 2004.

The Morocco mission in 2004 was a disaster on its own. The need for international rescue teams had been overestimated. Yet a political decision was made by the Icelandic government to dispatch a team since the prime minister had visited the King of Morocco just a few months earlier. As a result, the team had little work to do after they arrived in the country and flew back without feeling much had been accomplished.

The ICE-SAR team was made up of individuals from two of the larger rescue units in the capital area of Iceland. The current leader of the ICE-SAR team came from one of the units, and members from the other unit often felt decisions were being made without them being involved. This perceived division and the "wasted" mission to Morocco had led to morale going down drastically.

When I accepted taking on a leadership role I knew part of this background. Being originally from yet another rescue unit within the capital region, I felt that the team members might look at me as independent from this political tension going on. Little did I know, lot of my time over the following years would be spent dealing with that tension.

In this section we will look at different aspects of assuming leadership and discuss ways to address issues similar to those I experienced.

Becoming a leader: Chapter 6

Putting a Stake in the Ground

> That is what leadership is all about: staking your ground ahead of where opinion is and convincing people, not simply following the popular opinion of the moment.
>
> **Doris Kearn Goodwin**

First Impressions

Assuming a leadership position within an organization or a team is not always easy. This is especially the case if you take over an existing team, because you inherit all of the decisions and actions of the previous leaders, and all of the conflicts within the team that may or may not have been resolved.

I knew that I would have only one opportunity to make a first impression on the team of seasoned search and rescue experts that comprised the ICE-SAR team. I also knew that I had to be true to my principles and myself if I was going to fix the issues existing within the team. Finally, I knew that my appointment as team leader was not without controversy as they had expected someone from within the international USAR team itself to be appointed.

At the meeting where I was formally introduced to the team as the new leader, I decided to put a stake in the ground and be blunt about why I had accepted this position. This decision to air things out right from the start and to explain my goals and vision right up front was, in my opinion, the key to future success of the team.

I told the team that many of them knew me from my incident management area. I admitted to them that my knowledge of urban search and rescue (which focuses on how to break through walls of collapsed buildings in the aftermath of an earthquake to free people trapped under the rubble) was very limited. However, I knew how to lead a team, and I knew the international disaster environment that the team needed to work in.

I also admitted that I knew of most of the conflict and bad morale that had affected the team over the past few years. I explained to them that, in my mind, this conflict was now behind us. We were here to build up a new era of this team.

The international USAR community had created a set of criteria for what USAR teams had to be able to do in order to be able to call themselves an international USAR team. I told them my mission was to make the team one of the best urban search and rescue teams in the world and if they wanted to work with me on that vision, they should stay on the team; otherwise consider leaving it.

A number of the team members approached me afterwards, thanked me for my words, and said they were hopeful that things would change. There were, however, a few that approached me and started discussing things from the past; something I told them was no longer relevant.

Making Your First Impressions

You never get a second chance to make a first impression.

Anonymous

As you take on the role of a leader in a team or organization, make sure you research the history of the team. Try to uncover some of the conflicts and morale issues that the team is dealing with. If possible, make sure you get to hear both sides of the story. Hear from the old team leader and get their input on what works, and what does not work in leading the team. In addition, listen to the team members and hear their side of the story.

When you complete this research about the current state of the team, start developing a vision that you can leverage to bring the team forward. In my case, the vision I was going to leverage was that I was going to make the team the best USAR team in the world. Even though it was made up entirely of volunteers, I told them we were going to be the most professional USAR team the world had ever seen.

If possible, try your vision out on a few of the team members. Also, be sure that you have the support of your superiors to drive that vision forward. The last thing you want to do is to come across as someone with an unattainable vision or dream, because that vision is immediately shot down by upper management.

Further reading

- Built to Last by James Collins and Jerry Porras

Becoming a leader: Chapter 7

Dealing with the Past

> You build on failure. You use it as a stepping stone. Close the door on the past. You don't try to forget the mistakes, but you don't dwell on it. You don't let it have any of your energy, or any of your time, or any of your space.
>
> **Johnny Cash**

Ghosts of Leadership Past

Putting a stake in the ground and sharing your vision of the future is always a good first step as a new leader. However, it is crucial not only to make a good first impression, but also to ensure that the principles laid out during that first impression are what you will practice throughout your time as leader.

This can be particularly difficult when there are leadership "ghosts" that are "haunting" your team. Bad decisions made by previous leaders, or unresolved conflicts or tensions, can be difficult to deal with.

When it comes to "bad" decisions, team members often expect you to make the same decisions as your predecessor. Some of them will spend a lot of time "educating" you about these old decisions in order to show you just how "bad" those decisions were. The truth is, often those "bad" decisions were the best possible decisions that could be made at the time they were made, based on the available information at the time.

Over the coming years, I would often get long and winding phone calls, usually from the same few individuals on the team. They would talk about how things were, and how we were now at risk of making the same mistakes again. As a team leader, I felt it was important for me to listen, and let those individuals vent.

My answer to them was usually the same: "Thank you for telling me about the background of this situation. However, I want to remind you that I am not my predecessor, and we will now make decisions based on what is professionally the right way forward. We can't change the past, no matter how much we want to. We can ensure the future is one that helps make this team the best international urban search and rescue team in the world."

Different versions of this same answer were what team members heard me say over and over again, and as time passed, they understood that I was not there to try to exorcise the ghosts of the past, but to build a new future for the team.

Weeding Out the Bad Apples

> Anyone who has declared someone else to be an idiot, a bad apple, is annoyed when it turns out in the end that he isn't.
>
> **Friedrich Nietzsche**

Sometimes you face ghosts from the past that are simply too difficult to deal with. There will be cases when some of your team members are simply not willing to move out of the past, and no matter how many discussions you have with them, they simply refuse to focus on the future.

I am a firm believer in giving people an opportunity to change, but I also believe that it is important not to dwell on the past forever. You should not give up on people until you are sure you have done everything you could to help them change. But, if a team member cannot or does not want to move forward with the rest of the team, then the best option may be for that individual not to be part of the team moving forward. This is a key in building strong teams in the long term.

It is important to remember that no one is irreplaceable. They may have a long history within the team and be the best at what they do - but if their morale and behavior is such that they are creating damage to the rest of the team, then no matter how good they are, they should not be a part of your team.

Weeding out the worst apple(s) may also lead remaining "bad apples" to change and start moving forward, or they may choose to leave on their own accord. Your team may not have the same experience level for the short term, but in the long-term, the team will grow to become stronger and more effective.

Further reading

- Confronting Reality by Larry Bossidy and Ram Charan
- Crucial Accountability by Kerry Patterson, Joseph Grenny, Ron McMillan, Al Switzler, and David Maxfield.
- Crucial Conversations by Kerry Patterson, Joseph Grenny, Ron McMillan, and Al Switzler
- The Five Dysfunctions of a Team by Patrick Lencioni
- Overcoming the Five Dysfunctions of a Team by Patrick Lencioni

Becoming a leader: Chapter 8

Earning Respect

> The true test of character is not how much we know how to do, but how we behave when we don't know what to do.
>
> **John W. Holt, Jr.**

Respect Does Not Get Earned Overnight

As a new leader, it is crucial for you to earn the respect of your team members. Respect is like trust, something that takes time to earn, but can be tarnished in a matter of seconds. Putting that stake in the ground at the start is the first step in earning respect. How you deal with issues from the past can also help. However, it is important that your everyday actions continue to help you earn that respect.

How you respond to everyday problems or issues that come up will very much determine how quickly you can gain respect. You need to show that you are true to your vision in everything you do, but at the same time, you have to ensure you are not afraid to get your hands dirty and join the rest of the team in doing some of the heavy lifting when needed.

You Don't Know What You Don't Know

One of the best leadership lessons I learnt was one that we were taught at my first day at Microsoft back in 1998. It was the simple concept of "You don't know what you don't know." Admitting to others that you do not know something and say that you are going to find out is much better than pretending to know something you don't know.

This was definitely the case for me when it came down to the nitty-gritty details of urban search and rescue. I knew that the objective of the whole effort was to find people trapped in the rubble and then use tools to break your way through walls, floors, and ceilings to get that person out. However, I certainly did not know anything about the details of how to do that in a safe manner.

Right from the start, I admitted this to my team members. I told them that I fully trusted them to become the best in the world at breaking through concrete and that my role was to help them have the optimal conditions to work in. Admitting this shortcoming of my knowledge might sound counter-intuitive to earning respect, but in fact, it was one of the keys to me earning their respect. You cannot earn respect without showing respect. If you don't respect the expertise of others, they will not truly respect you.

I did not pretend to be something I was not. Instead, I relied upon them for information about how this aspect of our operation worked.

Admitting my lack of knowledge also gave me an opportunity to earn respect by asking them for guidance on how things worked. I could get my hands dirty getting lessons from them in the basics of urban search and rescue. A leader who seeks guidance from his members empowers them in sharing their hard-earned knowledge. At the same time, it helps them understand that even though you are a leader, you are not some all-knowing expert that can do everything by yourself. Also, it demonstrates that you see yourself as part of the team, not apart from it.

Let Your Actions Speak For Themselves

> You're going to come across people in your life who will say all the right words at all the right times. But in the end, it's always their actions you should judge them by. It's actions, not words, that matter.
>
> **Nicholas Sparks**

The old saying "you have to practice what you preach" is an important lesson in earning respect. If your actions are not in line with what you are telling others to do then you will not earn their respect.

Sadly, too many people, as they climb the corporate ladder, think they become more important than those who report to them. They think that the rules and principles they tell their subordinates to follow do not apply to them.

It is important to realize that it is often the small actions that irritate your team members the most and make you lose their respect. If you just stand and watch while everyone else is working hard on doing a mundane but important task, then they believe that you are not helping out because you feel you are too important to "get your hands dirty" helping out.

Be on the lookout for any opportunity to get down into the dirt and help with things that other leaders would not participate in and that will help you earn respect even faster.

Power Corrupts

> Because power corrupts, society's demands for moral authority and character increase as the importance of the position increases.
>
> **John Adams**

One of the worst examples of leaders losing the respect of their followers or subordinates is when they let their leadership role rise to their head and they start focusing on the power that comes with the role and stop focusing on the important task.

My grandfather always said to me "power corrupts." As he went to study in Germany in the late 1920's, he experienced the recession and the inequalities that people experienced. This led him to learn about communism and, when he moved back to Iceland after his studies, he became one of the founders of the Icelandic Communist Party. Through his long political life, he knew personally and met almost every communist leader in the 20th century.

He was still alive during the fall of the Berlin Wall and it was interesting to speak with him about this change. What surprised me most was his comment that there had not been communism in most of the Eastern Block for decades. He said that all of these countries had fallen into dictatorship because power had corrupted their leaders.

He was true to his values and as such he was the only leader of a communist party in the world to condemn the invasion of the Soviet Union into Czechoslovakia in 1967. This made him persona non grata in Moscow for quite some time. Also, during his almost 50 years in politics, he never held a position of power, such as a minister in a government, yet he was key to forming a number of coalition governments. All this because of his belief that power would corrupt and that he could do more work as the leader who brought people together.

Further reading

- The Influencer by Joseph Grenny, Kerry Patterson, David Maxfield, Ron McMillan, and Al Switzler
- The Trusted Advisor by David H. Maister, Charles H. Green, and Robert M. Galford
- Changing Minds by Howard Gardner
- Enchantment by Guy Kawasaki
- Influence Without Authority by Allan R. Cohen and David L. Bradford

SECTION 3

Building Resilience

Begin at the beginning and go on till you come to the end; then stop.

Lewis Carroll

Luckily, most of us do not have to take our team immediately into a crisis. For others, they may emerge as leaders of emergent teams that get created organically as the crisis develops. In this section, we will discuss how you can work on making your team more crisis proof, in other words a team that is more ready to take on the difficult tasks that it may have to deal with in the future.

Building Resilience: Chapter 9

The Importance of Resilience

> In order to succeed, people need a sense of self-efficacy, struggle together with resilience to meet the inevitable obstacles and inequities of life.
>
> **Albert Bandura**

Defining Resilience

Resilience is all about making things more ready to deal with and avoid potential difficulties ahead. There has been a strong tendency within the international humanitarian community to focus not only on how to prepare for future disasters, but also on how you can prepare communities that are at risk and make it easier for them to withstand the disaster. The same holds true for any team or organization. If you put focus on making the team more resilient to crisis, then it becomes easier for the team to withstand the difficult times that it may face.

There are many ways in which you can make your team more resilient to crisis. In this and subsequent chapters, we will focus on some of the key aspects.

It Takes Investment

> The leaders I met, whatever walk of life they were from, whatever institutions they were presiding over, always referred back to the same failure, something that happened to them that was personally difficult, even traumatic, something that made them feel that desperate sense of hitting bottom--as something they thought was almost a necessity. It's as if at that moment the iron entered their soul; that moment created the resilience that leaders need.
>
> **Warren G. Bennis**

Building resilience is not something that just happens overnight. It is something that takes time and investment. But just as we pointed out in the chapter on personal preparedness, disaster preparedness has a great return on investment – for every dollar you spend on it you will save six dollars of cost during the response.

However, making that investment requires long-term focus on resilience building instead of focus on short-term costs. This requires you to sell your long-term vision to your superiors so that they are willing to invest in it. That may take all your convincing power, but just remember it is definitely worth your while.

When I took over the ICE-SAR USAR team, we had set ourselves a goal. The criteria that the international USAR community had created for USAR teams involved a peer-based classification process, where 5-10 USAR team members from other teams would come and observe a 72 hour practical exercise where the team had to show its ability to meet over 250 different criteria.

We applied in 2006 for our team to undergo such a classification exercise in late 2009. The long waiting list to be classified, thankfully, gave us the ability to go through each criteria and identify ways to meet it. We discovered that although we could easily meet the "breaking through the concrete" part of the criteria list, there were a number of items on the list that required us to add capabilities and people to the team in order to meet the criteria.

Resistance to change

Do not follow where the path may lead, go instead where there is no path and leave a trail.

Ralph Waldo Emerson

As we started out the classification process, one of the common objections that I had to deal with was "but we have always done it this way, why change it?" This resistance to change is something you will encounter along the way of making your team more resilient and more able to handle the tasks in front of them.

When you face this attitude, it becomes important to explain in clear terms to those voicing it why we need to change what we do. The best approach to this is not to tell people how they need to change things, but to approach them with a particular problem. You then explain to them that you think that we are not going to be able to meet particular criteria the way we are currently doing things. Then ask them for guidance on how they would adapt the way we are currently doing things and get them to "own" the new approach. That way you do not have to convince them of anything because they become the champions of it.

Of course, this is not always possible and then being able to explain things clearly becomes your strongest ally.

Expanding the Team

One man can be a crucial ingredient on a team, but one man cannot make a team.

Kareem Abdul-Jabbar

Interestingly, one of the biggest issues that I had to face in building up the resilience in the team was when we discovered that the only way to meet particular criteria was to add new people and capacity to the team. Making those decisions was particularly hard, because not only did it require me to convince the existing team members that we could not simply add these as a new task for them to deal with, but I also had to convince our superiors that the costs involved in adding those additional team members was worth the investment it required.

In particular, there were two extensions to the team that were the hardest to get them to accept. The first was to add a special team to handle our base camp. In previous missions, the USAR experts themselves had been responsible for setting up a base of operations in the form of a tent camp where the team would sleep and eat.

Once the camp had been set up, in addition to working the physically hard task of breaking through concrete the team members had to come back to the camp and start making food. We pointed out that this caused our team not being able to do as much work digging through the rubble (a task that is very time sensitive since most people are found alive in the first few days of a disaster) because they were busy keeping their camp up and running. At the same time, they would not be able to rest as much in-between assignments and therefore would become more prone to accidents.

It only took one exercise for the team to understand the value of adding this unit to the team. The quickly discovered the "luxury" of not having to deal with logistical issues and got much better rest when all they had to do when they came back to camp was to clean themselves up and then eat the hot food awaiting them.

The second, more difficult, addition we made to our team was to add a group of experts that would have as their key role to interact with other teams and assist the United Nations in coordinating the overall response. The reason I pushed for the addition of this team was that the classification guidelines required that the first team to arrive in a disaster-affected country needed to set up the initial coordination of the rescue effort.

The pushback I got was mainly that we would never be the first team to arrive in a disaster area, so that we would not have to worry about this capability and that adding these four people to the team would incur additional costs, something our superiors were very cautious about.

I pushed, pushed, and finally got a green light from our superiors to add this unit, at least for the classification exercise itself. We therefore started identifying candidates for this unit and started training them. I was lucky that I was able to handpick people from our search and rescue teams that had years of experience in managing incidents and coordinating between teams. Even though they did not have any experience in USAR or the international disaster response environment, I knew that they would be able to do this task very professionally.

When the time came for the classification exercise itself in October 2009, my insistence on adding this unit paid off. The leader of the classification team, one of the most experienced disaster responders and coordinators in the UN said this unit had done their job so well that he would like them to consider offering their services to the UN as a stand-alone unit.

The main reason he said that was because he voiced his concern the unit would not be brought along to missions because ICE-SAR would never be the first team to arrive due to its geographical location. Only a few months later he had to "eat his hat" publicly to admit that statement of ICE-SAR never being the first team to arrive was very wrong. The ICE-SAR liaison and coordination unit did an amazing job in helping coordinate the USAR response in Haiti just as they had trained.

As you fight for the investment required to make your team more resilient and better able to deal with the crisis you may fight in the future, remember that even though it may take time and effort, it will certainly pay off when the crisis hits and you need that capacity. Make sure that you are pushing for capacity in the right places. It is easy to define a number of "what if" semi-realistic scenarios. Your real talent is to be able to select the critical set to focus on.

You may also want to consider the semi-agile approach we used within the ICE-SAR USAR team. We defined the team in a modular manner so that we could adapt it to different situations we might face. Not all of these modules need necessarily be part of the organization you lead, but they need to know how to integrate into your team in times of crisis.

Further reading

- Resilience by Andrew Zolli and Ann Marie Healy

- Antifragile by Nassim Nicholas Taleb

Building Resilience: Chapter 10

Crisis Planning

> Life is what happens to you while you're busy making other plans.
>
> **John Lennon**

Why Plan For Chaos?

You may ask yourself how you can plan for a crisis since it is bound to be a chaotic and unpredictable situation. The truth is that even though each crisis is different, there are a number of issues that are identical or at least similar enough that planning for them can give you an advantage.

In the disaster management world there is a long tradition of making plans. Most disaster management departments even have a person who focuses entirely on writing, testing and revising these plans. Within the corporate world, there has been a push over the last decade to introduce "business continuity planning," planning for how the company should deal with potential crises that may affect their ability to run their business.

The plans created vary somewhat but all of them have some things in common. They identify what triggers a particular plan to go into effect. They identify an organizational structure to use to manage the incident and they provide a set of processes that they follow to assess the situation, respond to the situation, and recover from the situation. Finally, many plans include a process for how to learn from the successes and mistakes that happened during the crisis response.

A Framework for Everyone to Work Within

There is a comfort in rituals, and rituals provide a framework for stability when you are trying to find answers.

Deborah Norville

A crisis response plan provides everyone with a framework to work within. No plan, however well-written, is good enough to predict everything that may occur, but it should be clear enough to provide guidance for how to tackle any issue that may come up.

It is therefore important that those who develop the plans make them flexible enough to act as a framework rather than a systematic playbook for how to deal with the crisis. An agile, well-written plan helps everyone know what their role is and what is expected of them.

It is also important that plans are not something that take a lot of effort writing, only to gather dust on the shelf. You need to go through the plan with your team and you need to exercise it (more on that in a subsequent chapter). When your team knows what is expected of them, they will be able to do their job so much better.

More Investment

Planning is bringing the future into the present so that you can do something about it now.

Alan Lakein

Creating a plan takes yet another investment. The effort of defining a crisis response plan is no easy task. Not only do you need to think through every process and every organizational chart, but you also need to discuss it in detail with those who actually are going to implement it and get their buy-in.

In our process of getting a classified as an internationally recognized USAR team, we went through this process. It certainly took a lot of evenings (we were all volunteers with day jobs) and a lot of discussions back and forth.

However, that investment initially paid off when we passed through our classification with very few remarks. And it really paid off when the real crisis hit on that cold January evening: The real reason why our team was able to become the first international team to arrive in Haiti was that when the call came everyone knew their role and followed the processes that had not only been written but also exercised a number of times.

Flexibility

> To exist is to change, to change is to mature, to mature is to go on creating oneself endlessly.
>
> **Henri Bergson**

As mentioned above it is important that any crisis planning you do is flexible enough to be useful as the chaotic environment of a crisis presents itself and looks totally different from what you had expected it to look like.

The best plans are meant to be broken someone said once. However, the best plans do not need to be broken because they should be flexible enough to be adapted to any situation that presents itself. They should provide guidance rather than nail down process. They should define the principles that must be followed, not systematic instructions for what to do.

Writing flexible crisis plans takes considerably more work than writing systematic instruction manuals, however, they stand the tests of time and chaos much better. They also help inscribe in those that are intended to follow them the right principles for making empowered decisions on how to proceed when a new fork appears in the road.

Further reading

- First Things First by Stephen R. Covey, A. Roger Merrill, and Rebecca R. Merrill

Building Resilience: Chapter 11

Everyone as a Leader

> Leadership is lifting a person's vision to high sights, the raising of a person's performance to a higher standard, the building of a personality beyond its normal limitations.
>
> **Peter Drucker**

Leaders Without Titles

I am a firm believer that no matter what title you have, you have an opportunity to show leadership in the work you do. One of my favorite authors, Robin Sharma wrote a book on this subject called The Leader Who Had No Title, which teaches us the importance of leadership at all levels of an organization through a fable about a lost soul who receives critical lessons about developing leadership qualities and skills at all levels of his professional and personal life, through meetings with five different people.

Leadership is in big demand when a crisis hits and often we look towards those with titles to show us that leadership. Unfortunately, not everyone has the leadership qualities needed to help us get through a crisis. Managers, for example may have risen up through the ranks in their organizations based on other reasons than necessarily their leadership qualities.

It is during a crisis that often we see the leaders without title rise up to the occasion and do amazing things. We often label those people as heroes. They do not give up when they face difficulties. They think outside of the box. They get others to help them achieve a common goal. They are willing to learn new things rapidly to reach a target. They are passionate about their work.

I have been lucky to know many such people that I have met through my work in crisis response. They are my role models when it comes to doing well. Interestingly they are also the people everyone wants to work with.

It may be strange that as people's titles become more important, sometimes their ability to show leadership becomes less apparent. I remember during one of my first international disaster response missions, where we were coordinating a joint assessment of a large flood area with the government.

I was put in charge of coordinating the assessment on behalf of the international humanitarian community and I walked over to the person who had been put in charge of the entire disaster response by the government.

I introduced myself and was about to provide him with information about what the international humanitarian community wanted to do, but before I could, he abruptly said to me "I will not talk to you. I only talk to your team leader." Unfortunately, this attitude was just a preview of his tone for the cooperation with the international community for the entire mission. To him, the chain of command and titles were more important than expertise or assigned roles.

In the humanitarian world, the real heroes are the humanitarian field workers, especially the local staff. These people go out amongst the affected community and give their all to help those in need. In addition, they bend rules and they find innovative ways to do things. They also collaborate with other organizations even though at the "leadership level" in those organizations there is competition.

In an earthquake response in Padang, Indonesia in 2009, I was fortunate enough to work with some real leaders. These were two female humanitarian workers, both from Indonesia, but working for the United Nations. If you looked at their title or their pay grade, you would have thought they were "nobodies." However, the truth of the matter was that these two women were the ones leading the collaboration between the government and the international community.

Without them, we would not have been able to provide assistance to the government of the affected country in the manner we did. It was a pleasure to work with them and interesting enough that particular disaster response has since been considered as one of the better-organized humanitarian response missions of the last decade.

What we need are more people like them, not only during crisis, but also in their daily job that are willing to rise to the challenge and drive leadership on a daily basis in everything they do – just think of what we could achieve!!!

As a crisis leader, it is important that you instill this culture of leadership at all levels of your team. During a crisis, you will not be able to monitor all of your team members closely and you must ensure that you have empowered them to act as leaders who follow the principles that you have laid down. They should not just get things done, no matter the consequences to others, but rather be flexible and get it done within a principled framework.

Growing Leaders

Before you are a leader, success is all about growing yourself.
When you become a leader, success is all about growing others.

Jack Welch

As mentioned earlier, one of the things we knew we had to address when I became a team leader for our USAR team was that our team was going to expand drastically in size. The classification guidelines for internationally recognized USAR teams, clearly specified what roles needed to be fulfilled in order to be classified as a team. This meant that our team, which previously had deployed sixteen people, now had to at least double in size. In fact, we ended up defining the ideal deployment size to be 34-36 people.

Since our USAR team is entirely made up of volunteers, we must always have at least three people for every person we need to be able to deploy internationally, since not everyone who is a volunteer will be able to leave at a moment's notice for two weeks, leaving work and family behind. This means that even though we would only deploy a 35-person team, we still had to have close to 100 volunteer members in the team, all trained in their respective specialties.

As the team expanded in size, specialization also grew within the team. This meant that we had certain members focusing on the urban rescue itself, while others focused on aspects such as logistics (setting up our camp and feeding the team during the mission), management (coordinating with other teams and planning the overall work), communication (establishing connection both to the teams working in the field and back home to Iceland) and medical (providing medical assistance to our team members as well as basic medical assistance to those we brought out of the rubble).

As a team leader, it became impossible for me to know each of these areas in details. It was therefore crucial for me to trust the expertise of those that I worked with. I would lay down the principles of what it was that was expected of their roles, but I left it up to them to define how they would perform their role.

All too often leaders end up micro-managing all aspects of everyone's work, because they are afraid that those working for them will not do things correctly. This becomes detrimental to morale within the team and people stop wanting to work for those people. They also do not try to do their best because they know that their manager will end up correcting them if they do something wrong.

When you develop a team of leaders, you develop a team that takes pride in the work they do and find innovative ways to achieve the tasks. You provide them with the principles that they need to adhere to, but you do not give them detailed instructions on how to do their job. This gives them a sense of responsibility and pride in doing their work, no matter how mundane it may be. It is crucial to respect and recognize this expertise others have, and it becomes even more important when you are leading people who can do their jobs better than you.

Yet not all roles that need to be done may feel as important as other roles. Being the person that digs someone out of the rubble may seem a much more important role than being the person who takes care of cleaning the camp and emptying the chemical toilets.

As the team grew in size, I ensured that I spoke individually with each of our 100 members, not in an office setting, but usually in the field during an exercise. In particular, I made an effort to speak to those that may have felt they had the mundane, less important roles.

I explained to them that each role in our team is of equal importance. Each of us plays a role in a well-oiled machine. Without someone taking care of the mundane and less glamorous jobs, we would not be able to save lives and work our way through the rubble.

I also made sure to explain this same thing to those who had the more glamorous jobs, that without others taking care of all the mundane things they would not be able to do their job as good as they were.

It took some time for this to leak into their consciousness, but after the first few exercises, they realized that together they were more powerful and each person became thankful for the roles each of them was playing.

This methodology is sometimes called "management by walk around" and has been cited as a characteristics of successful innovative leaders in a number of studies.

Leaderless Organizations

In the past few years, there has been a rise in organizations that have no leadership structure. The Occupy movement is probably the most well-known of these. These self-organizing organizations are often formed around a clear sense of purpose and principles. However, it is important to make a distinction between the fact that the organization has no leadership structure and the fact that people within the organization will take leadership in getting things done. Even the initial purpose and principles were most likely initiated by some leadership.

In fact, these organizations are practicing the concept of "everyone as a leader" described in this chapter. For these organizations it is important to clearly explain to participants the difference between the "everyone as a leader" concept and anarchy.

I have often observed when working with leaderless organizations a fear of making decisions. Participants do not want to be the ones making a decision, because of a fear of being branded as someone trying to take control of the organization. It is therefore important for these organizations to put in place some mechanisms that enable effective decision making, even if those mechanisms require someone to step up to the plate and guide/lead the organization through that process.

Suggested reading

- Primal Leadership by Daniel Goleman, Richard Boyatizis, and Annie McKee
- The Leader Who Had No Title by Robin Sharma
- The Leadership Challenge by James M. Kouzes and Barry Z. Posner

Building Resilience: Chapter 12

Leader of Leaders

> The leader's job is not to cover all the bases - it is to see that all bases are covered.
>
> **James Crupi**

Span of control

If your team consists of more than six people then you will have to delegate leadership to other designated leaders within your team because your span of control will not handle that many people. Nurturing and building those leaders within your team is essential for your success as a crisis leader.

In the US based Incident Command System (ICS), the term *span of control* is used to define the number of people reporting to a person. The span of control is key to effective and efficient incident management. Maintaining an effective span of control is important because safety and accountability are a priority.

> *Within ICS, the span of control of any individual with incident management supervisory responsibility should range from three to seven subordinates. If a supervisor has fewer than three or more than seven people reporting to them, some adjustments to the organization should be consid-*

ered [illegible] *five subordinates.*

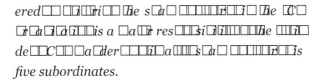

FEMA ICS-200 Independent Study Course

Over the last few years we have seen a trend within many organizations to go for a more flat hierarchy with large numbers of people reporting to a manager. Although this may have some benefits from an organizational management perspective, this can be very difficult to work with during crises, since you just don't have the luxury of time needed to be that much of a bottleneck to operations. You may therefore decide to have a more rigorous hierarchical structure in place for times of crisis.

Leaders Reporting to You

The leaders who work most effectively, it seems to me, never say "I." And that's not because they have trained themselves not to say "I." They don't think "I." They think "we"; they think "team." They understand their job to be to make the team function. They accept responsibility and don't sidestep it, but "we" gets the credit. This is what creates trust, what enables you to get the task done.

Peter Drucker

If you are lucky, then you can pick those people who will be the ones assuming these role of unit or "squad" leaders within your team. In other cases, such as in my case with ICE-SAR, those leaders will already have been chosen as they represent the managers of a particular department or unit.

No matter which case you end up having, it is now your task to grow these leaders and help them develop as leaders. I've already mentioned two of the best ways you can do this, being a great role model for them and to get your direct reports to rise up to the role that they have assumed by empowering them to do their work the way they feel is most appropriate, as long as they are following the principles and values you have laid out.

In our USAR team, we had six different sub-units each with a designated unit leader. Each unit leader represented a particular specialty, such as medical, camp operations, communications, etc. Due to us being volunteers, each unit actually had 2-3 unit leader "candidates" who would assume the unit leader roles depending on whether they were available for the particular mission or not. This meant that I had in fact a total of 12-18 possible unit leaders that I had to develop and nurture.

Each of the unit leaders was then responsible for a unit consisting of anywhere from 2-8 people.

Empowering Unit Leaders

The more I help others to succeed, the more I succeed.

Ray Kroc

As we will explore in more detail in a later chapter, one of the key ways I used to build a great rapport with them and help them rise to the challenge was to empower the unit leaders. I did this by telling them that I was no expert in their field of specialty and that I would rely on them to run that part of the mission.

The analogy I used was that the whole team was a puzzle and without all of the pieces working properly, we could not achieve our goals. I told them that I trusted them to ensure that their piece of the puzzle was working at their best and through that, we would achieve building the world leading team we set ourselves out to become.

Each unit took this challenge, some took it sooner than others, but in the end they all ensured their piece of the puzzle was part of an overall well oiled, well-functioning team.

Training Unit Leaders

In order for the unit leaders to ensure that their piece of the puzzle works great, you also make them responsible for ensuring that their unit trains for their function. However, what is often forgotten is to provide specific training for the unit leaders in how to lead small teams.

It is sometimes expected that just because someone becomes a manager of a unit then they actually know how to lead a team. Even if they have gotten some management training, in very few cases have they received any training in how to lead a team during a crisis.

It is therefore important that as you build up the resiliency of your team you ensure that you include specific training and exercises for your unit leaders. This investment will certainly pay off during your crisis response.

You should sit down with your unit or squadron leaders regularly and discuss openly with them the progress they are making. Don't just focus on the work they are doing. Take time to discuss their leadership development, how they feel they are progressing as leaders and how you can better support that development. Discuss with them leadership challenges they have faced and give them your feedback on how they might address those.

Depending on the person, you may need to do this quite often, while for others, you only need to do this every once in a while. Remember that this task of developing your leaders is just as important as you leading the overall team.

Dealing With Unit Leaders Who Can't Lead

Leadership is the challenge to be something more than average.

Jim Rohn

The same holds true for unit leaders as it does for any other member of the team. If you discover that someone who is a unit leader due to his or her status in the corporate hierarchy, and does not have the capacity to lead, then you should deal with that issue as quickly as you can.

One of the best approaches is to sit down with the person and discuss the situation openly and fairly. Ask them whether they are actually enjoying their management role or if they ended up getting into that role because that was the only way to get better compensation.

Many companies discovered during the late 1990's that the typical way of rewarding good employees by promoting them into management was counter-intuitive. They discovered that many people were not meant for management. They enjoyed their individual contributions towards their work, but not the added responsibilities of human resource and financial management.

Microsoft Corporation was one of the first companies to create a separate "engineering career ladder" which allowed the company to recognize and reward individual contributors without having to make them managers. This allowed them to take some of the smartest engineers and give them compensation and rewards similar to what a General Manager or VP got without adding responsibilities of managing other people.

Sadly, not all organizations have these dual ladders for individual contributors and managers. This means that you will find people in unit management positions that do not have the drive or interest in managing or leading other people.

If you are dealing with this, then try to find ways to help this person become an individual contributor again without losing their ability to rise within the company. Then work on identifying replacements that have the drive and interest in leading other people.

If however the unit leader simply is one of the bad apples that refuse to adapt to change, then find ways to get that person out of the team and identify a good replacement that will help effect the needed changes.

Further reading

- Leaders Eat Last by Simon Sinek
- A Leader's Legacy by James M. Kouzes and Barry Z. Posner
- Leaders Open Doors by Bill Treasurer

Building Resilience: Chapter 13

Exercising

Repetition is the mother of all skills.

Anthony Robbins

Why Exercise?

A common way of training and building resilience is to take your team through an exercise. In an exercise, your team members are put into a simulated environment and have to deal with situations that they may potentially face when a crisis it.

Exercising your crisis plans and your team is one of the most effective ways to make your team resilient to crisis. This is done by simulating a crisis incident and go through the thought process it would normally have to go through during a real life emergency. This allows you to develop your leadership skills under low-consequence and potentially low-stress conditions.

Running an exercise also allows you to try out your crisis plans and identify issues with the processes and organizational structure you have created. It allows you to identify areas of training that need to be focused on and it allows you to monitor how your unit leaders and you handle the stress of leading in a time of crisis.

Different Types of Exercises

There are a number of different types of training exercises that can be used to test out your crisis plans. One of the easiest ones to run is what is known as a tabletop exercise, which we will explain below. You can also go full force into a realistic role-playing exercise that attempts to fully simulate the crisis environment.

You can run different types of exercises to focus on different aspects of your team. Some exercises may focus on exercising the overall function of the team, while others may focus on exercising the leadership aspects of the team. Below we will look at different types of exercises.

Tabletop Exercises

A tabletop exercise can be held anywhere without too much investment, except in time. In a tabletop exercise, you usually exercise and test the leadership organization and processes, as well as coordination and cross-team dependencies.

In a tabletop exercise, you bring the team and unit leaders into a conference room big enough for everyone and with some basic supplies such as whiteboards and/or flipcharts. You then have an exercise facilitator run the tabletop exercise by injecting situations into the exercise, in the form of new information becoming available to the team, at predefined moments.

In the beginning of the tabletop exercise the participants are given an overview of the overall crisis they face and they are told to start responding according to their predefined processes based on the limited information they are given.

As they go through their processes they receive injects that they then need to react to. Some injects are not meant to change the overall direction of the crisis response but simply provide information or sometimes confuse the situation further. Other injects are specifically created to force decisions from the leaders at various levels and their response to those injects is then recorded by the facilitator and discussed in a debriefing at the end of the exercise.

A tabletop exercise usually runs for a couple of hours and at the end of the exercise there is an immediate debrief of everyone as to the issues they identified as needing to be further looked at and also to point out things that did go well. At the end of this debrief, the facilitator and, potentially, observers share their findings, which often provide new insights since they see things from outside the team itself.

Role Playing Exercises

Another type of exercises often used are full-scale roleplaying exercises, which require much more effort to plan and run. Because of this, most full-scale roleplaying exercises will last for hours or days as various aspects of the crisis response plans are exercised.

When you plan to run a full-scale exercise, you usually select a group of people that will act as the exercise control. They are responsible for defining a complex scenario, identifying a location to run the exercise and find people to play the various roles that will be used to deliver injects into the scenario as it progresses. Running a large scale exercise is also a great way to learn, because you get to act as an observer to everything that happens and as you plan the exercise, you come up with various conditions that the team might encountered. Both of these make you go through the thought process of what would be the best approach to deal with each situation.

Similar to the tabletop exercises, the team leadership is initially presented with a crisis that they are asked to respond to. The difference is that while in the tabletop exercise everyone gathered around a table in a conference room, here people are expected to act their role out in the location in which they would perform it if this were a real situation.

In more complex scenarios, the exercise control may actually be required to find an environment that can be used as a simulated crisis environment and then direct the team leader to move the team there at the appropriate time for the remainder of the exercise.

The exercise control will also rely on people to provide injects instead of simply handing over paper slips or issuing verbal cues. These "actors" therefore provide the exercise control with an ability to not only provide information in one direction, but also actually simulate a bi-directional interaction that can be adapted more readily in response to the participant reactions.

As in the tabletop exercises, role-playing exercises also end with a debriefing where feedback is given on lessons identified during the exercise. It is important to use this opportunity to identify mistakes that need to be corrected, because if we don't correct them, then we will perform as we have practiced and the exercise simply reinforced wrong behavior.

Practice Makes Perfect

No matter which type of exercise you decide to run for your team or organization, it is certain that the investment will pay back greatly when next you have to deal with a crisis. Each time you run an exercise, each of the participants identifies ways that they could perform their role better.

Running exercises also helps your team become better prepared for the chaotic environment that they will have to face when a crisis strikes. In particular, they will be better prepared mentally to deal with the difficult issues that they need to solve and can rely upon experiences from the exercises as basis for those solutions.

Further reading

- Emergency Management Exercises by Regina Phelps
- Applied Crisis Communication and Crisis Management by W. Timothy Coombs
- Crisis Leadership by Ian Mitroff

SECTION 4

When Crisis Strikes

Sooner or later comes a crisis in our affairs, and how we meet it determines our future happiness and success. Since the beginning of time, every form of life has been called upon to meet such crisis.

Robert Collier

No matter how much we prepare, the crisis always strikes when we least expect it and it usually manages to be different from anything we have faced in the past. It is in these initial moments of crisis that leadership becomes critical. In this section, we will look at those critical moments and how you as a crisis leader can react to them.

When Crisis Strikes: Chapter 14

Your First Reaction

> You can't relate to a superhero, to a superman, but you can identify with a real man who in times of crisis draws forth some extraordinary quality from within himself and triumphs but only after a struggle.
>
> **Timothy Dalton**

The Moment a Crisis Strikes

Your first reaction when a crisis strikes sets the path for how you deal with it moving forward. If your emotional reaction is one of anger, fear or despair, then you have to deal with that reaction carefully before you can start doing anything else.

It is quite easy to let a number of emotions flow through when a crisis strikes. Your mind is filled with questions such as:

- Why is this happening?
- Why did this have to happen to me/them?
- What will this mean for my/their future?
- What will this mean for my family?
- Why did they do this?
- Will we/they ever recover from this?

It is quite natural to ask yourself these questions. They are all closely linked to the six human needs we discussed earlier. Very often, a crisis strikes so close and the severity of it is so big that we start to question our own values and believes. Those that are religious may ask themselves "why would God let such a terrible thing happen?"

The key to your success as a crisis leader is that, once that initial reaction has passed, you quickly do the self-analysis we discussed earlier and look at how you reacted and why. Once you have done that, you can start preparing for taking the next steps, which require you to step up as crisis leader.

You as an Affected Leader

Faced with crisis, the man of character falls back on himself. He imposes his own stamp of action, takes responsibility for it, makes it his own.

Charles de Gaulle

Many crises do not only affect those around you, they affect you yourself, and you are one of the "victims" of the crisis. This can influence how you deal with the crisis in more ways than you would expect.

When you yourself are affected, you need to overcome your own grief or loss so that you can step up and lead the overall community or organization you are tasked with leading out of the crisis.

Just as we have numerous examples of people who have put their own loss to the side and risen to this challenge, we have even more examples of people who have simply given up and not been able to rise to the challenge. It is difficult to say what separates those two groups of people, but it is my opinion that it is in big part based on their own preparedness, resiliency and the experiences they have gone through prior to the crisis striking.

At the same time, it is also essential for those who rise to the challenge and start leading the crisis effort to realize that the time will come when they will have to deal with their loss and grief. Although many find helping others a way to mask those emotions, they have not gone away and still need to be addressed at some point in the future. It is important that you have in place a mechanism for discussing those emotions and feelings when that point comes. When the opportunity arises, you also have to be willing to step aside and deal with your own issues, and let others assume leadership.

Activate your Family Emergency Plan

Expect the best, plan for the worst, and prepare to be surprised.

Denis Waitley

As we discussed earlier, it is important to have a plan in place for how the family will deal with you being away leading the response to a crisis. Now that the crisis has struck, it becomes important for you to activate this plan. Remember, the sooner you can let your spouse know that a crisis has struck, the more time you give your family to make all the necessary arrangements.

Try to give them an estimate of how severe this crisis is and when they can expect to see you next. Be as realistic as you can and tell them the basics of the crisis, without causing them to become worried about you or themselves.

Finally, tell them you will contact them again a set time from now and then set an alarm/reminder to remind you of reaching back to them. Even if it just sending a text message every few hours, it keeps things at home within control. This also helps you as a leader to keep yourself grounded and reminding you that there still is a larger world out there.

For the Greater Good

Successful people recognize crisis as a time for change
- from lesser to greater, smaller to bigger.

Edwin Louis Cole

While your ability to rise to the challenge and start leading during a crisis depends on your ability to deal with your own sense of loss and grief, it is also important for you to keep a clear focus on your role as the crisis leader.

Sadly, there are too many examples of crisis leaders that have put their own needs in front of the needs of the greater good. They have worried more about how to recover their own loss than they have about how to solve the needs of the many. The converse can also be found, where people denied their own needs to a point they are not making good leadership decisions.

During the financial collapse in Iceland in early October 2008, a small number of people in the banking sector caused the country to become technically bankrupt. They had taken more and more risk in order not to deal with bad investments. They thought that they could borrow money forever, but when the international lending market dried up after the collapse of Lehman Brothers, then their dominoes started collapsing.

Instead of working together collaboratively and leveraging their assets and networks to find ways out of the situation, their focus was on how to save themselves so that they could keep up their high standard of living. During the last months, weeks and days before the collapse, they started ignoring their values and principles and started making deals and transactions whose only purpose was to get cash out of the system before it all collapsed.

As leaders of large financial companies with hundreds of thousands of employees worldwide and as leaders responsible towards tens of thousands of shareholders, they stopped looking at the greater good and focused on saving their own skins.

Their "raid" on the system was so bad that, in early October 2008, the Central Bank of Iceland did not have any currency reserves. The last few dollars that the bank had were used to pay for the trip of the finance minister to the World Bank/International Monetary Fund annual meeting in Washington DC where he was tasked with finding support from "friendly countries" to prevent the country from going bankrupt.

The situation was so dire that a team of employees in the Central Bank were called into work on a Saturday morning to find ways to establish an emergency bartering system with foreign countries because no foreign currency was available to pay for imported necessities such as oil, food, and medicine.

Over the preceding weeks, many of those who knew of the impending crisis had visited their bank branches and changed all of their cash into foreign currency. They walked out with briefcase after briefcase of US Dollars, Euros, Yen, Swiss Francs, and British Pounds. Ordinary people planning to travel out of the country were shocked when their bank branch told them that all they could get in foreign currency was $50.

Thankfully, through personal relationships between a high level person within the Icelandic Central Bank and a high level executive within JP Morgan, a channel was kept open for exchanging Icelandic Crowns (now worth half what they were worth before that difficult day in October 2008) into US Dollars.

In a great example of what personal leadership between people in two organizations could achieve in times of crisis, this "hole" through the system was what saved Iceland from total collapse and rationing of necessities.

Further reading

- Emotional Intelligence 2.0 by Travis Bradberry and Jean Greaves
- Emotional Intelligence by Daniel Goleman
- The Brain and Emotional Intelligence by Daniel Goleman
- The Emotional Life of Your Brain by Richard J. Davison and Sharon Begley

When Crisis Strikes: Chapter 15

Keeping Calm

Knowing yourself is the beginning of all wisdom.

Aristotle

Don't Panic – Keep Calm

One of the most important qualities a crisis leader must have is the ability to keep calm in the middle of the chaos. As the uncertainty of everything becomes ultra-high, you still need to be able to make decisions and get things done. As all kinds of emotions run through your brain, you need to be able to put them on ice temporarily and focus on the tasks at hand.

The act of keeping calm and not panicking in the face of a crisis is the ultimate test of your ability to focus. Your ability to keep calm is being challenged by your emotions trying to overtake your rational thinking. Your ability to focus is affected when everyone around you is panicking and losing hope. It is also affected when you experience things you may never have experienced before.

During the crisis, you need to keep your focus on four key tasks. First, your task as a crisis leader is to find ways out of this crisis. Second, your task is to help others deal with the crisis. Thirdly, your task is to think outside the box for solutions to the complex issues you are facing. Last but not least, your task is to get others to follow your example and empower them to face the crisis.

Preparation

> Good fortune is what happens when opportunity meets with planning.
>
> **Thomas Alva Edison**

Your ability to keep calm during a crisis is highly dependent on how well you have prepared yourself for dealing with a crisis. In the last section, we talked about a number of factors that you need to focus on to be more resilient. It is at this point, when the crisis strikes, that you get the reward for all that preparation effort.

The more self-awareness you have developed, the better prepared you are for dealing with the emotions and feelings that you will experience in the times of crisis. Your ability to digest those emotions and feelings and choose your reaction to them is critical for keeping calm.

The more exercises you have participated in, the less foreign are the situations that you experience. Although the exercises are never 100% realistic, there are parts of them that you will experience again when the real crisis strikes. You will already have thought through some of the problems you are about to face, even if it was just for pretend.

Panicking Doesn't Get You Anywhere

> A leader or a man of action in a crisis almost always acts subconsciously and then thinks of the reasons for his action.
>
> **Jawaharial Nehru**

One of the key things to keep in mind is that panicking really does not get you or anyone else anywhere. Panicking is a primal response that helps us deal with immediate threats. As the lion jumped in front of the cave dwellers, panicking helped them run away from the threat.

However when the threat faced is not a lion that will eat you, but "simply" a set of problems that need to be solved, then panicking doesn't get you anywhere, except to more problems.

You must be conscious of this primal emotion and ensure that, when you experience panic, you interrupt that thought process by reminding yourself of the importance of your role and keeping calm.

But I Am Not the Calm Type

Those that know me through my disaster work might think that I am always a calm type that keeps focusing on the tasks. What they do not know is that, as a kid, I was the hyperactive type. I was a kid that got into trouble every week, sometimes every day. Today, I would probably been diagnosed with ADHD or something along those lines and given some cocktail of drugs.

Thankfully, I did calm down a bit as I got into my teenage years, but I certainly am not the quite calm type that you would think I was based on seeing me handling a disaster. When a crisis strikes, my focus becomes very clear. I know that it is my role to help lead us out of this crisis and, if I panic or do not keep calm, then things will simply not work as well. Therefore, I put lot of effort into keeping that focus and not letting my emotions control me.

Letting Off Steam in a Controlled Fashion

Does this mean that I never raise my voice in a crisis? No, but it actually happens very seldom and only when it is really called for and when I know that raising my voice will have the intended consequence.

During our mission in Haiti, my team came to me because the team that had set up camp next to us was being very loud. It was actually not the team itself, but a group of reporters and other media staff that had come with them. These media people insisted on doing live broadcasts from Haiti late in the evening at the same time as most teams were going to sleep.

I first explained calmly that our team members had been working in the field for eighteen hours and needed those few hours of sleep before they started up again. I felt they showed utter disrespect, especially by saying that they still had two hours left of their broadcast.

I then asked them who their leader was. Initially, they refused to tell me. When I pointed out to them, in not so calm terms, that I would disconnect their power generators on the spot if they did not bring me to their leader, they finally took me to her.

After waking her up, I explained things calmly to her and pointed out that they brought media people into the middle of the rescue team camp and this was not acceptable. I also told her that we understood they were in the middle of a live broadcast so we would be willing to let them finish that in the next 20-30 minutes, but anything longer than that and we would exercise our authority as camp managers not only to turn everything off but kick the media out of the camp.

She quickly explained to her friends from the media that they would have to cut their work short to give our team members rest and fifteen minutes later, they had finished their broadcast and turned everything off. The next morning they also moved all their equipment out of the camp so that they could do their work without interrupting the rescue teams.

Could I have done this calmly and not raised my voice? I tried that first, knowing my own team members had tried speaking with them earlier. When the response I got back was utter disrespect, I used some of my bottled-up emotions. Afterwards, I felt a little sorry for them, because I knew that I had not just vented my anger about their disrespect to them, but also let go of some built-up steam from dealing with difficult things over the last few days.

So, choose your battles wisely. Know when to use your emotions and when to keep them at bay. If possible, do not use them against your own team members or those that you are working with, because it is hard to mend burnt bridges.

Further reading

- Focus by Daniel Goleman
- Don't Sweat the Small Stuff and It's All Small Stuff by Richard Carlson

When Crisis Strikes: Chapter 16

Role Model for Others

> A leader is one who knows the way, goes the way, and shows the way.
>
> **John Maxwell**

Everyone Is Looking at You

Being the leader means that you become the center of attention and people look to you for guidance on how to overcome the crisis ahead. It is therefore particularly important for you to act as a role model for those around you, especially your team. This can be difficult, especially if the crisis affected you directly.

Acting Like You Know What to Do

> You don't lead by pointing and telling people some place to go. You lead by going to that place and making a case.
>
> **Ken Kesey**

It is a common mistake to think that a leader needs to act tough in order to be a good role model for those around them. A true leader knows that showing compassion is not a weakness, but a sign of strength. A true leader knows that asking others for their input is a sign of intellect and not of weakness. A true leader knows that the most important task is not to panic and instead face the challenges.

In times of crisis, true leaders help to calm those around them. They seek guidance from their team before making the most difficult decisions and act as role models to others by not panicking. In times of crisis, true leaders appear calm, even when, inside they are struggling to keep their fear of the unknown at bay.

Expectation Setting

Never tell people how to do things. Tell them what to do and they will surprise you with their ingenuity.

George Patton

As you start promoting the vision of hope for the future it is very important that you keep setting expectations correctly. You must ensure that you are not making promises you can't keep. You must be realistic, especially when it comes to the time factor.

A common mistake in managing a crisis is to be too optimistic when it comes to when things will get better. Many of us have experienced waiting for a plane that has mechanical issues. An experienced pilot will inform the passengers early about the potential issues causing the delay and will explain why and how this issue will be addressed. An experienced pilot will also be realistic about the time it may take to fix the problem.

An inexperienced pilot might not inform the passengers that there is a problem until after the planned departure time has passed. The inexperienced pilot will often not explain in detail what the issue is. The inexperienced pilot might also not update the passengers regularly about the progress in fixing it.

A true leader knows that if you are open about the issues faced and if you set expectations realistically, then people's trust in you will grow, because they feel like the leader is addressing the issues at hand in the best way possible.

On October 6, 2008 the prime minister of Iceland made a television address to the country, telling everyone that Iceland was about to go through a very difficult financial crisis that would have severe consequences. He ended the address with "God bless Iceland," a sentence that set the stage for people's mood for the coming weeks.

While the whole nation was in shock, very few understood how serious the situation really was. Not only were all of the banks in Iceland doomed to end in bankruptcy, the central bank had run out of all foreign currency and England, where its gold deposits were kept, was putting Icelandic banks on the terrorist watch list in order to freeze their accounts. If it hadn't been for personal contacts with JP Morgan bank, through which currency trades could be made, the country would have been closed to all foreign currency transactions and basically not been able to import food, fuel, medicine and other essentials.

For a country that had experienced the highest standard of living in the world, this was a terrible setback. That high standard of living had been made possible through loans that people could not afford to pay back. Everyone was living in the dream-state that there would always be a way to pay when the loans were due. This was true in the business world as well as for families.

With the prime minister's initial television address, people's expectations had been reset. In many ways, it was a cold gush of water thrown in their face. In the next few weeks, everyone watched as each bank tumbled and the currency was halved in value. Politicians were helpless and did not know what to say to people other than "there is a crisis."

People became restless and demanded change. They took to the streets and protested. After a while, the politicians listened and elections were held. Those parties that were in power lost seats while those that were in opposition got more seats than they had before because people expected that they would run things differently.

However, as time passed, how did it all go? The banks were resurrected with help from the government and although many companies have gone bankrupt, many of the large companies have been taken over by the banks. Those companies were kept alive while they were being "restructured."

Many people lost their homes, but a much higher number of people have been kept on "life-support" by lowering their monthly payments while extending their debt way beyond the original loan periods. This holds true for both car loans and mortgages.

However, where the new government really failed was in setting expectations. By dragging their feet to face the consequences of the bad loans and the beyond-capacity lifestyle, they got people to believe that they would get through this without losing their houses or cars. They made people believe that they would need to cut down their spending on luxury items for a few years, but, after that, everything would be fine.

Almost 18 months after the fall of the banks, the legal system ordered that a large portion of car loans and mortgages established in Iceland since 2003 were actually illegal. They had been tied to foreign currency rates, but that practice was found to be illegal. After this judgment was issued, people were left in a vacuum for over two years while the decision of how to recalculate the loans went through the legal system. During this whole period, people were given the hope that they actually might not owe very much on their expensive cars that they could not afford to buy in the first place and maybe they might be able to keep them.

In the meantime, the government did not do much to address the needs of those who were going to lose their housing. Their message was always that they would "help the families," but they always pushed any action of doing so towards the resurrected banks. Moreover, if asked what was being done, government leaders always said the banks were offering many options. The truth of the matter was that the banks were actually only assisting a very small portion of the affected households.

What can we learn from all of this? The main lesson is that, when your ability to deal with the situation is limited, then you have to set expectations low. You have to brace people for the inevitable and help them get through those times in as good way as possible. Yet you have to make them understand that they will not have the same kind of life as before.

If, however, you set their expectations too high and tell them that everything will be all right, then you are bound to fail. A golden rule is to under promise and over deliver, i.e. set expectations low and then deliver more than you promised. That way you keep people satisfied with what you are doing – because, even if we wanted to, we cannot perform miracles.

However, this is something politicians have a hard time doing, because it is seldom good for votes to tell the truth and explain to people what has really happened and what they are really going to face. Instead, it is much better to make promises that underneath you do not know if you can keep, but at least you have 4 years to try and people are good at forgetting what you said 4 years earlier.

This is something that many crisis managers understand and after a disaster has struck, they often warn people that things might get worse than they actually will get. "We might get strong aftershocks" or "The flooding might get worse before it gets better" are sentences you will hear from crisis managers while "we hope the worst is over" and "we will get you back home as soon as possible" are sentences the politicians will be saying.

Therefore, if you are tasked with making public statements during or following a crisis, make sure you set expectations low. If things get better than you expect, then you can always claim that it was due to the good work of your people. If, however, you set expectations high, your job is on the line and you most likely will lose it.

Further reading

- Who Will Cry When You Die? by Robin Sharma
- The Story of My Experiments With Truth – M. K. Gandhi
- Long Walk to Freedom by Nelson Mandela

When Crisis Strikes: Chapter 17

Preparing for Difficulties Ahead

In a crisis, don't hide behind anything or anybody.
They're going to find you anyway.

Paul Bryant

Focus on the Long Term While Solving the Short Term

It is crucial to remember that a crisis usually is not solved overnight. As a leader you have to remember that you are in it for the long term. Remember, dealing with a crisis is more like running a marathon rather than running a 100 meters sprint.

Sadly, too many leaders forget this long-term focus and overdo it during the first 24-48 hours. Going on without sleep and running on adrenaline and endorphins (or energy drinks) is an easy recipe for failure.

It is therefore important for you to start right away preparing yourself for the marathon ahead. You will need to set yourself some guidelines for how to ensure you are able to perform for the long run.

But I Need to Lead at All Times

There cannot be a crisis next week. My schedule is already full.

Henry A. Kissinger

One of the most common misconceptions is that, as a leader, you have to be in command at all times and therefore you cannot afford to rest. This is particularly true during the turbulent chaotic times of a crisis. It is however important for you to realize that, if you try to lead all the time, then your decision making will deteriorate radically as your lack of sleep starts affecting you.

It is important for you to set yourself rules that limit your operational periods. This is a common practice in the disaster management field, where the need to pace responders has been well understood for quite some time. There each day is split into a set number of fixed-length operational periods or shifts, for example three eight-hour operation periods or two twelve-hour periods. This is also a common practice on ships, airlines, and other fields.

If you are leading during one of the operation periods, then you need to find someone to take your place during the other operational period. If you are uncomfortable with empowering them to make all the decisions during their operational period, then be clear about what decisions you are willing to let them make and give them guidelines for when to wake you up for critical decisions. That way you can achieve some rest, while at the same time keep control of the most critical decisions.

Stop and Listen to Your Body

I am not my body. My body is nothing without me.

Tom Stoppard

It is important for you to listen to your body throughout the crisis operation. When it starts failing you in some ways, then it is a clear sign that you need to rest more. Do not forget that rest also means eating and drinking plenty of liquids (and not just caffeine drinks).

In 2000, the World Trade Organization (WTO) held its annual meeting in Seattle. The police had expected some protestors, but the large number of protestors that arrived and the fact that a number of anarchists infiltrated the protests and turned them violent surprised everyone.

I was part of a volunteer team that assisted in the county's emergency operation center at that time. On day five or six of the protests, when everyone had been working almost non-stop since before the meeting started, one volunteer member arranged for a group of massage students to come into the operation center and give everyone a short massage.

It was amazing, even to me, to see the effect this little bit of relaxation and focus on improving the state of everyone's body had. This rejuvenation enabled everyone to continue working for the remainder of the mission.

Further reading

- True North by Bill Geroge and Peter Sims
- Sergio by Samantha Power
- The Four Agreements by Don Miguel Ruiz
- The Greatness Guide by Robin Sharma

When Crisis Strikes: Chapter 18

Keep Yourself Grounded to Reality

> Close scrutiny will show that most 'crisis situations' are opportunities to either advance, or stay where you are.
>
> **Maxwell Maltz**

Remembering What It Is All About

If you are not directly affected by the crisis, then in the midst of a crisis, it is easy to forget why you are really responding. As your focus is on the high-level issues, you often forget that there are people at the receiving end of the problem you face. These people are living the real crisis. They are experiencing all the chaos first hand. The crisis has affected them personally much more than it has affected you.

Rich Serino started his career as a paramedic in Boston and over the next three decades became one of America's most respected emergency managers. He was recruited in 2009, shortly after retiring, to become the deputy director of the Federal Emergency Management Agency (FEMA).

As second in command at FEMA, Rich regularly sits down with survivors of natural disasters in shelters. His reason for meeting with the survivors is not that he wants to show them that FEMA really cares, but rather because he wants to understand first-hand how the work that he is leading is affecting those who bear the brunt of the crisis.

Within hours of Hurricane Sandy passing over New York, he was visiting the affected areas. At 1 am in the morning, after a long day of surveying the devastation, Rich insisted on visiting a shelter and sitting down with survivors. In a shelter in New Jersey, he met with a few survivors who were glued to a television showing images from the area.

To break the ice, he asked them if they were Giant fans. Himself being a die-hard Red Socks fan, that gave them a mutual ground to connect. A few minutes later the discussion turned to the crisis and the experience the survivors had just gone through. Feedback he got during this discussion would greatly impact FEMA's response in the days and weeks to come.

An experienced crisis leader like Rich knows that it is crucial to remain grounded with reality at all times. The best way to achieve that is to connect with the people experiencing the crisis first-hand. It is very easy to get lost in aggregated operational details that speak of 10,000 people affected or 50 people dead or hear an organization's spokesperson talk about a caseload of 50,000 people. Sitting down with the relatives of those who died or meeting with the survivors provides you the right perspective to address the issues at hand.

Under the leadership of Rich Serino and his manager Craig Fugate, FEMA has changed their approach from a top-down crisis response model to what they call survivor-centric response. Putting the survivors at the center of everything they do - something that of course is met with resistance by those who like the status quo - is part of improving the country's crisis response and making it more effective.

Leading from Ivory Towers

When they come downstairs from their Ivory Towers,
idealists are very apt to walk straight into the gutter.

Logan P. Smith

To those most severely affected by a crisis, it often feels as though those leading the response live in ivory towers. In these ivory towers, process trumps innovation and sending reports to donors or superiors trumps actual action. They feel that those leading think that everything you are doing is more important than what is happening on the ground. To those leaders numbers are more important than individuals.

Sadly, way too often we see leadership attempted from inside the ivory towers. During the financial collapse in Iceland in 2008, many of the politicians tried to solve the crisis from within the parliament. They were afraid to speak directly with the people who were worst hit by the crisis. Growing discontent caused the general public to start protesting outside of the parliament, but still few politicians dared to go outside to talk with people.

Dorrit Moussaief, the wife of Iceland's President, Ólafur Ragnar Grímsson was an exception to this. During the formal start of the parliament sessions in the fall of 2011, she left her husband's side as he and the members of parliament walked from the parliament over to the national cathedral for a mass. The police tried to stop her from climbing the fences that kept the protesters at bay, but to no avail. While members of parliament and ministers in the government sat in the ivory tower of the cathedral, she spoke with the protesters.

Even though she holds no power and even though many looked at this incident as a comical farce, the truth of the matter is that she showed true crisis leadership, by reaching out to those who were disgruntled, while most of those in power continued to lead from afar.

Emotional Drain or Emotional Recharge?

A smile on a missing child reunited with its parents is what keeps me volunteering for search and rescue at all hours of the day.

Gisli Rafn Olafsson

Many leaders, not themselves directly affected by the crisis, are afraid to interact with those most affected by the crisis. They are afraid to face the emotions of the people. They are afraid to make the response personal. This may be because of an old fable that, in order to get through difficult times, you must distance yourself from the terrible things that have happened.

I firmly believe that in order to respond well to a crisis you must connect very closely with reality on the ground. In my two decades in search and rescue, the most rewarding role I played was to be the liaison between the rescuers and the family of the missing person. Many would think that meeting people in this highly emotional time would be very emotionally straining. It may be so for some, but for me it was a time of recharge. This emotional recharge came from a heightened focus on my reasons for doing the work I was doing.

You can control your mind's response to seeing or hearing about the effects of the crisis. You can let your mind go even further into despair or you can use it to strengthen your resolve to help find an innovative and successful way out of the crisis. A true crisis leader always aims for the second option.

Personalize the Crisis

Personalizing the crisis is a very effective way to sharpen your focus, but you can also leverage it to help those you lead sharpen theirs. This is something successful leaders have utilized throughout the ages to gain support for their vision.

The only way you can truly personalize a crisis by telling someone's story is if you have actually met the person you use as the lead in your story. Having held their hands and truly felt the emotions they are experiencing will shine through as you tell others about the situation that they are facing.

Sadly, many think they can skip the uncomfortable step of actually meeting the person. They think they can leave that to the responders on the ground. They think they can simply retell the stories that they hear from them.

However, when you take that difficult step and actually connect with a survivor, you remind yourself first-hand why you are doing this. You help yourself sharpen your focus and every time it wavers, you can put the image of that person in your mind and your focus automatically goes back to the key issues you are facing.

Listen and Then Act

We have two ears and one mouth so that we can listen twice as much as we speak.

Epictetus, Greek Philosophers – AD 55

When you meet with those affected by the crisis, it is crucial that you actively listen to what they are saying. Truly hearing what they have experienced and what they are experiencing will shape your understanding of the crisis, as nothing else will.

Let your mind capture not only what they are saying, but also the emotion and body language associated with it. Refrain from trying to compose a response to what you are hearing while they are still talking. In an emotional situation like this, for them to see that you are truly listening is worth more than any words that you can say.

To them it is also natural that you will need some time to process your response to what they just told you. Actively listening and responding a short period after they have finished speaking has the effect on them that they truly feel listened to.

As you respond, make sure to start by reinforcing what they just told you. Not only does that show them that you truly listened, but it also gives you a little more time to formulate your response. As you respond, try to make them feel that you genuinely care about the situation they are facing.

Very importantly, do not make promises that you cannot keep, because these will only burn you later. Show them empathy with their situation and explain to them that you will certainly use their input to determine actions to take moving forward and if possible you will try to follow up with them.

Once you have met with them, formulate in your mind and with others, how you can address the most critical issues that these people raised. Focus on finding solutions that are scalable, not only to the situation of the individuals you met, as well as to all others that are in similar situation.

Further reading

- Execution by Larry Bossidy, Ram Charan, and Charles Burck
- Victory in Our Schools by John Stanford
- It Takes a Village by Hillary Rodham Clinton

SECTION 5

Decision Making in Chaotic Environments

> A true leader has the confidence to stand alone, the courage to make tough decisions, and the compassion to listen to the needs of others. He does not set out to be a leader, but becomes one by the equality of his actions and the integrity of his intent.
>
> **Douglas MacArthur**

When we make decisions we do so based on the information, we have at hand, our experience and our "gut feeling." In times of crisis, we rarely have all the relevant information at hand and we may never have experienced the particular situation before, so all we have to go with is our "gut." Or is it?

In this chapter, we will start by looking at the role information plays, how we gather it, how we process and analyze it and how that affects the decisions we make. In subsequent chapters, we will then look at how to deal with uncertainty and failure as well as the role protocols play in helping us to make decisions when we lack the appropriate information to make a good decision. Finally, we will look at the concept of "thinking outside of the box" to come up with innovative solutions to the problems at hand.

Decision Making: Chapter 19

Role of Information

No one is without knowledge except him who asks no questions.

West African Saying

Why is information relevant?

Noise becomes ***data*** when it has a cognitive pattern. ***Data*** becomes ***information*** when it's assembled into a coherent whole, which can be related to other information. ***Information*** becomes ***knowledge*** when it's integrated with other information in a form that is useful for making decisions and determining actions. ***Knowledge*** becomes ***understanding*** when related to other knowledge in a manner useful in anticipating, judging and acting. ***Understanding*** becomes ***wisdom*** when it's informed by purpose, ethics, principles, memory and projection.

Dee Hock

The statement above, made in 1996 by Dee Hock, the founder of Visa Corporation is one of my favorite quotes related to information and decision making. It so clearly defines how we use information to make rational decisions.

For crisis leaders, it is crucial to develop the skills to find patterns in the noise, assemble a coherent whole out of the data, integrate information together to make it useful for decision making, relate knowledge to other knowledge to make it useful for anticipating, judging and acting and, finally, informing understanding by purpose, ethics, principles, memories and projection.

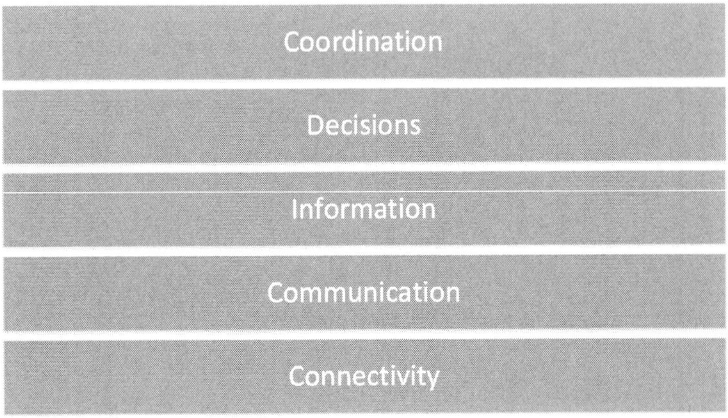

Figure 2 - The Role of Information

As the figure above shows, then information is at the center of our ability to really drive successful response to a crisis. In order to be able to coordinate the response, you need decisions to be made. These decisions are based upon information that is communicated over some mechanism of connecting the different responders together. If any layer in this "coordination stack" is not working, then it affects all the other layers.

In this chapter, we will look at some of the key principles in travelling down this path and discuss what issues often arise when you try to collect the right information in a crisis.

The Crisis Information Paradox

> Information itself is very directly about saving lives. If we take the wrong decisions, make the wrong choices about where we put our money and our effort because our knowledge is poor, we are condemning some of the most deserving to death or destitution.
>
> **John Holmes, former UN Emergency Relief Coordinator**

When a crisis hits, information about it is usually very limited. At the same time the demand for information is extremely high, because everyone wants to know what can be done to respond to the crisis.

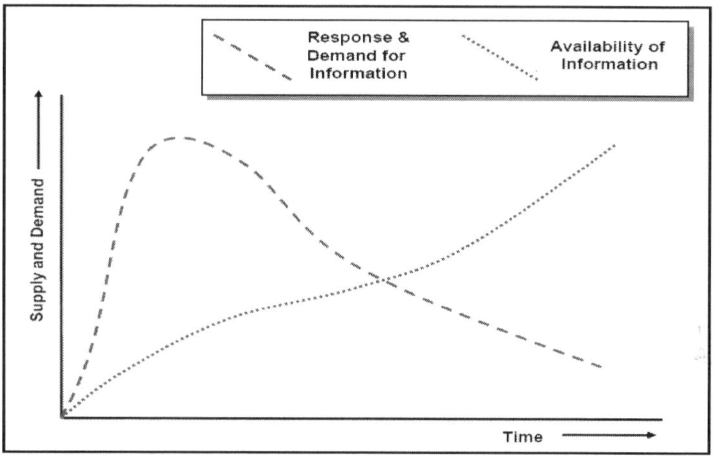

Figure 3 - Crisis information paradox. Figure courtesy of the United Nations Office for the Coordination of Humanitarian Affairs (UN OCHA).

This relationship between supply and demand of crisis information is depicted in Figure 1. What this diagram tells us is that, when the need for information is the highest, the supply is at its lowest. As the availability of information becomes greater, the demand actually goes down. It is therefore very important for us to prioritize closely what information we seek to gather, especially in the first phase of a crisis when our ability to gather it is also in short supply.

Although this is the case in most crises, the opposite can also be true. In today's information-rich environment, we may be faced with overflow of information. Too much information is often more difficult to deal with than too little because filtering out all the noise can be a more difficult task than gathering the missing information.

What Information Do I Need?

Crisis leaders such as disaster managers, have experienced a significant change over the last few years when it comes to getting information. Previously, they would rely on verbal reports coming in over radio from first responders in the field. The information from the first responders is then utilized to create a better awareness of the overall situational (often expressed on a map), thereby allowing decision makers to be better informed when they start making decisions.

In today's social media environment, images, text, and videos of the situation are being provided in real-time from citizens on the ground or near the incident. With this rapid influx of information, the key question becomes how to select which information is needed to make better decisions?"

Work Your Way Back

The first thing you need to do is to list out what decisions you are trying to make. Once you know what decisions you want to make, you need to define what information you would use as the basis for making these decisions. Once you know what information you would use as basis, then you can start thinking of how you can gather data and through data processing and analysis turn it into the needed information. You should also look at what is the best way to represent that information to optimize decision-making.

This leads you to ask more controlled questions instead of trying to capture all the available data out there and finding random ways to make decisions based on a flood of data.

Prioritizing Information Gathering

During a crisis it is often not possible to wait until you have all the information you think you need before you make a decision. Furthermore, not all information gathered may be actionable, and in crisis management, collecting information that is not actionable is a waste of time and resources. It therefore becomes necessary to prioritize what data you collect, process and analyze into actionable information.

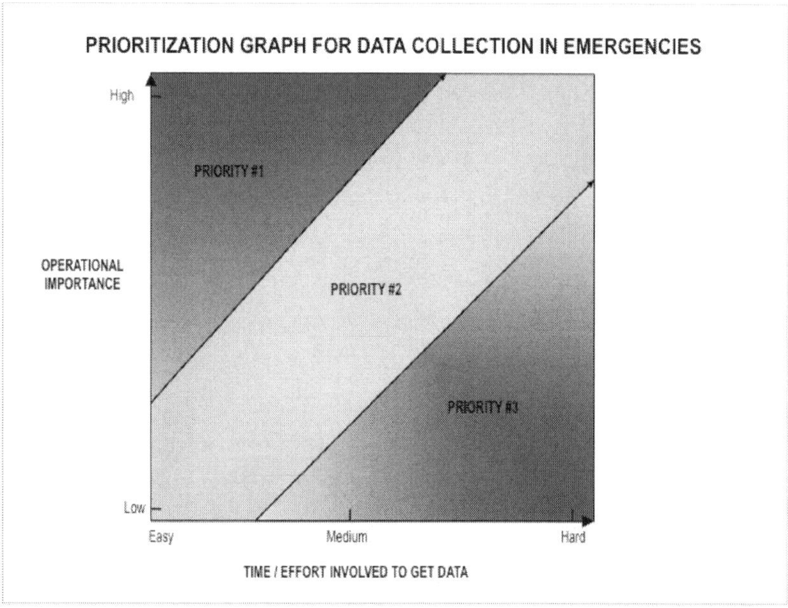

Figure 4 - Prioritization graph for data collection

The information management officers at the United Nations High Commissionaire for Refugees (UNHCR) developed the prioritization graph in Figure 4 to help people prioritize what information to focus on collecting.

In the initial phase of the crisis, it is important for us to focus on gathering information that is easy to get and that has high impact on our crisis operations. As time passes, we move the focus to information that is a bit more difficult to gather, but has medium impact on our crisis operations.

With the help of this graph you can prioritize which information to focus on gathering at each phase of the crisis. It enables you to focus on gathering actionable and relevant information. Sadly that is a step that often gets forgotten in a crisis and time gets spent on gathering information that has little impact on the crisis operations or information that is difficult to gather receives prioritization over information that is easier to gather yet has similar or even higher impact on the crisis operations.

Breaking Down Barriers

As a crisis leader, you have to break down any barriers that may exist between people or organizations that stop information from flowing freely. In a crisis, many decisions are made without the appropriate information needed to make a rational decision. Sadly, leaders often find out that the information they needed already existed, but had not been shared.

There can be many reasons why information is not shared. The reason may be political in nature. An organization does not want to share particular information with another organization because they feel that the information gives them an advantage in responding to the crisis that the other organization would otherwise have.

The reason may be technical if the information is in a format that makes it difficult for the organization to share it. Finally, it may also be a capacity issue, the organization simply does not have enough manpower to focus on both capturing and sharing the information in an effective manner.

Your role as a crisis leader is to identify the issues stopping information from flowing freely and to diffuse them. Doing so may require you to leverage your personal relationships with the other organizations and to help them see that sharing the information is a step toward the common goal of addressing the crisis. These issues may be political, technical, or capacity related.

Information may not be flowing freely because organizations or people are unwilling to share them since they feel having access to it may give them an advantage over you. Getting them to share the common vision of dealing with the crisis is often the best way to break down these political barriers.

Information may also not be flowing freely because of technical issues. How you share the information, may make it hard for others to use it. These barriers can be addressed by agreeing upon formats and processes for sharing the information in a standard manner.

Information may finally not be flowing freely, simply because the other organization or person may not have the time or expertise required to share it with you. Helping build up information management capacity before a crisis strike is the best way to avoid the capacity related barriers.

Further reading

- The Signal and the Noise by Nate Silver
- The Information by James Gleick
- Crisis Information Management by Christine Hagar
- The Power of Habit by Charles Duhigg
- Predictive Analytics by Eric Siegel

Decision Making: Chapter 20

Dealing with Uncertainty

Knowledge is an unending adventure at the edge of uncertainty

Jacob Bronowski

Welcome to the World of Uncertainty

The process of decision-making can be viewed as the task of reducing uncertainty of possible solutions by gaining better knowledge of the options at hand and thereby enabling an optimal selection of options.

In times of crisis you are bound to have to deal with great uncertainty. Things are changing so fast all around you that it is impossible to get a comprehensive overview of the situation. Your ability to make a decision under highly uncertain conditions is one of the key skills you need to develop. The option of waiting for all uncertainty to disappear is not a reasonable choice, but, sadly, often seen when people become paralyzed with the difficult task at hand.

Our emotions, especially fear and anxiety, play a key role in how we experience the uncertain environment of a crisis. It is important for us to expect and acknowledge that these emotions, especially fear of failure, loss or rejection, will influence how we address uncertainty. The sense of losing control of your life or being perceived as not being in control is a very unsettling one and it will affect your decision-making ability.

In this chapter we will look at steps you can take to deal with uncertainty in times of crisis. The ideas, suggestions and theories presented in this chapter come from various sources and are based on state-of-the-art research in the area of decision theory.

Location of a Base Camp

One of the first decisions I had to make for our team in Haiti after we landed was where we would set up our base camp and coordination center. During our reconnaissance of Port-au-Prince during the first evening, we looked at a number of options for setting up a base camp. One included a sport stadium, but it was already occupied by over 200 survivors of the quake.

After evaluating all of the options around Port-au-Prince, we decided we would set up our base of operations within the airport perimeter, mainly because it minimized the risk factor of having our equipment and supplies taken. It also provided plenty of space for additional arriving teams, which we knew would be numerous.

Even though this decision meant longer times for us to travel to the worst affected part of town, it also allowed us to have all the rescue teams located in the same area, something that was invaluable for coordination purposes when over 60 teams and 1500 rescuers had arrived within the next few days.

Classical Decision-Making

Nothing is more difficult, and therefore more precious, than to be able to decide.

Napoleon Bonaparte

For many decades, it was believed that decision making was all about defining a rational process. That in order to make good decisions we needed to separate emotions from rational thinking. The ancient Greeks believed that since humans are rational, so when they make decisions they are supposed to consciously analyze the alternatives and carefully weigh the different pros and cons.

Using this model it would be normal to split the decision-making process into the following steps:

- **Problem Definition** – describe the problem and opportunity at hand.
- **Background** – what is the historical information pertinent to making the decision?
- **Describe the situation** – what is the current situation and what is the information you have gathered?
- **Alternative solutions** – define the alternatives you have and qualify each one
- **Recommendation** – define the rationale behind your decision

The problem with this approach is that during a crisis, the knowledge of the external factors becomes very limited and the extremes of the possible values for the external factors becomes greater. This severely complicates the application of classical decision theory.

What is even more important is that this rational decision making model is not how the brain works. Many decisions, especially those made in response to a crisis, are made as a visceral reaction to difficulties ahead. These visceral reactions are based upon emotional impulses that are programmed into the neural network of your brain. Every feeling that goes through your brain is really a summary of data, a visceral response to all of the information that can't be accessed directly.

In order to make good decisions, we must leverage both parts of our brain, the rational part and the emotional part.

Use the Information at Your Fingertips

Information is the resolution to uncertainty.

Claude Shannon

In the last chapter we looked at the importance of information. One of the keys to reducing your fear and anxiety on making a decision is by learning enough about the options you have at hand before you make the decision.

The ability to grasp the key aspects quickly becomes crucial when making decisions during a crisis. You do not have time to read through long reports, so you must be able to skim through them quickly and pull out the key issues. This requires you to have a good background information about the issues at hand, but it also requires you to be able to focus on the forest and not the trees. During a crisis, there is a lot of detailed information that will be thrown your way. You need to be able use this input to build a view of the overall picture and use that to make decisions.

A good crisis leader will put an emphasis on collecting just enough information and having a team that helps analyze the crucial big picture items out of the influx of details.

Minimize Risk

A peacefulness follows any decision, even the wrong one

Rita Mae Brown

You should avoid any unneeded risk that you can. The fewer variables that you have to deal with the better. You will always have certain aspects that are under your control and you can ensure that you minimize risk in these areas.

Instead of making big decisions, break the decision down into smaller steps, where you can evaluate your options at each stage. This minimizes the overall risk of failure, because you can adjust your approach as the uncertainty reduces.

Be aware of the fact that no crisis is without risks and being a good leader is the ability to minimize the risk while at the same time being willing to take the risk associated with making imperfect decisions.

Be True to Your Goals and Values

Life is the sum of all your choices

Albert Camus

Always try to be authentic in your decision-making. Make decisions that are in line with your principles, goals, and values. There is a reason your values have guided you so well through your life. Doing the right thing, even if it is the difficult thing always results in a better outcome than doing the easy thing.

Following your values will also help you to justify a wrong decision later. This is especially true when you need to justify your decision to yourself. We all make wrong decisions, but if we firmly believed we were making the best decision possible at the time we made it and we followed our values, then we can live with our mistakes. Remember that you couldn't have been anyone else at the time you made this decision. It was based on your values and principles and those are unique to you.

Clarify the Consequences

> In any moment of decision the best thing you can do is the right thing, the next best thing is the wrong thing, and the worst thing you can do is nothing.
>
> **Theodore Roosevelt**

You need to understand the consequences of your decision as clearly as possible. Know what the potential gains and losses are from making the decision. One good approach is to understand what the worst-case scenario is for your decision. If the worst case is something you are willing to live with, then you can use it to limit your fear.

If the worst-case scenario is bad enough for you not to want to have it happen, then take smaller steps that limit your exposure to the worst-case consequence. This way you can find the baby steps needed towards a resolution without taking too much risk.

When deciding where to put up the base camp, the worst case scenario for setting camp up at the sports stadium, was that all of our equipment would be taken away while we were out in the field, leaving our team not able to continue our mission. To me, that was unacceptable.

The best-case scenario is often too good to be true. The final result usually lies somewhere in between those two extremes. We often call that the most likely scenario. Understanding all three of those scenarios helps you get a better picture of what the consequences of you decision will be.

The Cost of Doing Nothing

> When you have to make a choice and don't make it, that is in itself a choice.
>
> **William James**

It is also important to understand the consequence of not making a decision and to understand why you are not making a decision. If the reason for not making a decision is simply that you fear making it, then this should raise red flags within yourself. If, however, the reason is that you don't have all the required information, then that should cause you to seek out the missing information instead of giving in to the fear.

However, it is crucial to understand that you will never have all the information you need to make the perfect decision. Some of your decisions will be wrong (more on that in the next chapter). You need to be able to take that golden path in between having all the information and having no information.

To understand when better the time is right to make a decision and when the time is right to wait, it is important to factor into the equation the consequences of not making a decision. As you go through the different options in your decision, consider the risk and the cost of the "do nothing" option. Understand that the cost of doing nothing changes with time and you must reevaluate it at every step of the way.

Further reading

- The Black Swan by Nassim Nicholas Taleb
- Thinking, Fast and Slow by Daniel Kahneman
- Nudge by Richard H. Thaler and Cass R. Sunstein

- How We Decide by Jonah Lehrer
- Sway by Ori Brafman and Rom Brafman
- Blink by Malcolm Gladwell
- The Art of Choosing by Sheena Iyengar
- The Paradox of Choice by Barry Schwartz
- The Power of Habit by Charles Duhigg
- The Tipping Point by Malcolm Gladwell
- Incognito by David Eagleman
- Made to Stick by Chip Heath and Dan Heath
- Drive by Daniel H. Pink

Decision Making: Chapter 21

Dealing with Failure

Good decisions come from experience. Experience comes from making bad decisions.

Mark Twain

Nobody is Perfect

One of the biggest barriers to success is the fear of failure. This is especially true when decisions need to be made. We become so overcome with the fear of making the wrong decision that we resist making any decision.

It is important for us to understand that nobody is perfect and nobody makes the right decision all the times. The important thing is not to avoid ever making wrong decisions, but to learn from making wrong decisions. If you never learn from your mistakes and make the same wrong decisions again and again – then you are a failure. If you learn from them and don't repeat your mistakes – then you are successful.

When is the Right Time to Stop?

There are no failures – just experiences and your reactions to them.

Tom Krause

Our first day in Haiti was a long but very rewarding day. In the first hour of operations within Port-au-Prince we had rescued two women out of the rubble of the Caribbean Supermarket. We then spent the next ten hours freeing a woman stuck in a small space in the middle of the rubble of the supermarket. We could hear her call for help and we could talk to her, but it took us a long time to find exactly where she was. When we finally did we brought her out safely. This was televised live on CNN.

But we knew that there had been more than 150 people in the supermarket at the time of the earthquake and that only a handful had managed to run out when the earthquake hit. As the rescuers searched through the rubble, they came across many bodies of people who had been crushed to death.

Outside the supermarket, a large group of relatives had gathered hoping that we would find their loved ones. Some of them had been searching by hand in the rubble before we arrived and some claimed to have heard from their loved ones through mobile phones and text messages, even though the mobile network was not operating.

When the rescue of the third woman was completed, our team regrouped and started planning the search for further survivors. We had been joined by a Spanish rescue team that specialized in bringing rescue dogs to earthquake areas. Our team therefore performed a combined search of the rubble using both the Spanish dogs as well as high resolution listening equipment specially designed for searching in rubble.

The team spent a couple of hours repeating the search, both using the dogs and the technical devices. No matter how well they combed through the rubble, there were no signs of life. Yet the reports from the relatives gave us an indication that more people might still be alive.

After discussing things with my search manager, we decided to check if there were other rescue teams in the area. Our colleagues from the USA Task Force 1, which is made up of very experienced USAR experts from Fairfax, Virginia, were nearby and we got one of their search team squads to come over and perform a detailed search using their technical equipment.

They searched the rubble for about an hour and their result was the same as ours. No signs of life. Based on this information, I went out to the crowd and explained that, based on our searches, we could not hear any signs of life, but that we would not consider this site to be fully searched and would therefore recommend to those coordinating the overall effort that a new team would be sent there the next day with a fresh set of ears and eyes.

The relatives were not very happy to hear that we were leaving, but with the team very tired after performing search and rescue operations for close to twenty hours it was clear our team needed rest and telling the relatives we would get another team to continue helped calm them somewhat.

Before we left, we marked the building using spray-paint, something all international USAR teams do in order to let other teams know of dangers in the building and what had been found there. One key thing we did was to mark the building as "still needing more search."

The next day a team from Turkey came to the site and, after tunneling (crawling through the rubble), could hear signs of life. Over the next thirty-six hours they found five more people alive in the rubble, all of which they brought out successfully.

Two days after we had been at the Caribbean Supermarket, I learned about the additional rescues. To me it was a big shock. We had made a decision not to continue searching because we had not heard any signs of life. Yet we had left more people alive in the building than we had brought out.

Many years earlier, when learning to become an incident manager in search and rescue, I had been told "all decisions, made on the basis of the best available information at the time of decisions are the right decisions, even if found later to be the wrong decision." I reminded myself of this and said that our decision to stop searching could be justified, because we didn't say the building had been fully searched and we recommended that new teams would be sent there the following day.

What became even more difficult for me was whether I should tell the team about this. I knew it would have devastating effect on the morale of the team, so I took a couple of days before I told them and in the meantime I found out more facts about where the additional survivors had been found, who had found them and I actually spoke with the rescuers involved.

When I finally explained the situation to the team, I made sure to give them credit for the lives they had saved that day. I also made sure to emphasize our decision not to mark the site completely searched and, finally, I emphasized the fact that we had suggested sending new teams there the following morning. All of this had led to the rescue of these people from the rubble.

It still was very difficult for the team to come to grips with the fact they had left people in the rubble. But instead of focusing on the "failure," we focused on how we could use this as a lesson to search even better and to improve the team's technical search capabilities in the future.

Learn as Long as You Live

I didn't fail the test, I just found 100 ways to do it wrong.

Benjamin Franklin

It is important for us to use each failure as an opportunity to learn. Knowing that we will continue to make mistakes simply means that we have an opportunity to continue learning as long as we live.

The first time you make a mistake, consider it a lesson. The second time you make the same mistake, consider it a reminder. The third, fourth or fifth time you make the same mistake – then you are allowed to consider it stupidity.

Analyze why you made the decision that led to the mistake. In your mind consider what drew you towards that decision. Was there some missing information or information that I should have sought that would have made you make a different decision? How could you have ensured you had access to that information? Was there information that was there that I ignored or didn't understand fully?

The key to learning and improving is to take responsibility for the "failure." If information is "missing," you can blame it on others. If you failed (for whatever reason) to obtain information you needed, you only have yourself to blame. Of course, if you tried to get it and couldn't, then you can ask whether you exhausted alternative options. If you did, then you can honestly claim that you did your best and that was the best you can do.

Those are the kinds of questions you should be asking yourself. Questions that help you improve your future decision making process. These will help you prevent making those mistakes again in the future. Asking them is much more productive than asking any question starting with "What if..." or lingering on thoughts starting with "If I only..."

Never Giving Up

Dealing with failure means never giving up. It means moving forward even when things get tough. The following excerpt from Paulo Coelho's book Manuscript Found in Accra puts it elegantly:

> You managed to finish what you began even though you did not foresee all the traps along the way. And when your enthusiasm waned because of the difficulties you encountered, you reached for discipline. And when discipline seemed about to disappear because you were tired, you used your moments of repose to think about what steps you needed to take in the future.
>
> You were not paralyzed by the defeats that were inevitable in the lives of those who take risks. You didn't sit agonizing over what you lost when you had an idea that didn't work.
>
> You didn't stop when you experienced moments of glory, because you had not yet reached your goal.
>
> And when you realized that you would have to ask for help, you did not feel humiliated. And when you learned that someone needed your help, you showed them all that you had learned without fearing that you might be revealing secrets or being used by others.

Further reading

- Outliers by Malcolm Gladwell

- Derailed by Tim Irwin
- The Invisible Gorilla by Christopher Chabris
- Celebrating Failure by Ralph Heath
- The Logic of Failure by Dietrich Dorner
- Adapt by Tim Harford
- Failing Forward by John C. Maxwell
- You are Going to Fail! So Get Over it! by James Weaver
- The Power of Failure by Charles C. Manz
- Mistakes Were Made by Carol Tavris and Elliot Aronson
- The Wisdom of Failure by Laurence G. Weinzimmer and Jim McConoughey

Decision Making: Chapter 22

Following Protocols

> Don't necessarily avoid sharp edges. Occasionally they are necessary to leadership.
>
> **Donald Rumsfeld**

Preparing a Path through Difficult Times

In a previous chapter, we discussed the importance of making preparedness plans that help us deal with the chaotic times of a crisis. These plans not only help us define processes to follow, but also outline protocols and rules for us to follow. It is difficult to emphasize enough how important this preparedness work is. Using the analogy from disaster risk reduction, one can say that, for every hour you spend on creating these preparedness plans, you will save six hours during a response.

Having clearly defined operating procedures to follow during times of crisis enables us to make decisions quicker based on those protocols. The different options and decision paths have already been discussed, analyzed and thought through and the protocols define for us the path that in most cases will lead to the best outcome.

We must, however, remember that protocols are optimized towards a particular predefined situation and that the current situation we are in may point us towards other options than what the protocols suggest.

All Rules Are Meant to be Broken

Emergencies override laws.

Old Icelandic Saying

The old saying that all rules are meant to be broken was undoubtedly created in the midst of a crisis. Rules and protocols are often created for normal times. We may have invested in creating emergency protocols, but, still, these were developed with a particular situation in mind, one that we are not facing. We must therefore always be ready to adapt our decision-making in ways that may break the protocols we normally follow. When we do so, we must be very confident in why we made that particular decision.

The better you understand why the protocols are the way they are, the more opportunity you have in making an informed decision for not following a particular protocol in times of crisis. The more involved in making those protocols and rules, the more informed you will be. If you were not the one who created the protocols, be inquisitive and ask those who did. Make it your task to be well informed about the whys behind the protocols.

When you consider breaking a protocol, make sure you have made a well-informed decision. Make sure to document your reasoning, because in all likelihood those are the decisions people will question you about. Get a second opinion from someone you trust, if you can. Explain to them why you are making this decision and see if your reasoning holds. If it does and you still feel comfortable about breaking protocols, then inform everyone clearly that you are making a decision that breaks protocol and give them the reasoning, so that they are going to be willing to implement your decision.

Of course, there will always be protocols and rules that you should not break, no matter what. These are the protocols and rules that are clearly aligned with your core values and beliefs. Going against those will never be right whether it is in your heart or in other people's minds.

Rescuing People or "Borrowing" Fuel

One of the problems of travelling by air to a disaster zone is that you are not allowed to bring any fuel onboard the airplanes for safety reasons. You are actually required to ensure that all of your equipment that uses fuel, such as generators, is totally emptied of all fuel remains.

This meant that when we landed in Haiti in the afternoon of January 13th, we arrived with no fuel at all. One of the first tasks we had to do while searching for a suitable location for our camp was to find a source of fuel for our heavy rescue equipment and generators.

As we drove through the streets of Port-au-Prince, we realized that there was not a single functioning fuel station in the city. In the protocols of the international urban search and rescue community (International Search and Rescue Advisory Group - INSARAG), it is the responsibility of the affected government to provide fuel to the arriving teams. The problem was that most of the government was non-functional due to the massive destruction.

After looking for fuel and a place to camp, we returned back to the airport late in the evening. By that time, the US military had arrived and we put on our biggest puppy eyes and smiles to ask them for a few liters of fuel. They broke their protocols and gave us a couple of small fuel tanks. Sadly, we discovered quickly that the fuel they gave us did not work properly on our generators, because it was a mix of gasoline and diesel.

We dispatched two groups to search for fuel. One went out on one of the trucks that the national civil defense had allocated to us and they drove a circle around the airport looking for a fuel station that might have some fuel available. This team came back empty-handed.

Meanwhile, the other group, which included me, went walking around the airport with few empty fuel cans and a hose. Knowing that we were in an airport, we were certain that there might be some fuel available that we might be able to "borrow."

As we wandered around the airport, we found a lot that had been fenced in at some time in the past. It was filled with equipment from Air France. In there, we saw a beat-up Jeep Wrangler that obviously had not been driven in years since all four tires were totally flat. I told the guys with me to check if there was any fuel in the fuel tank of the Jeep.

The Jeep was actually almost full of fuel, so, using a technique all search and rescue team drivers in Iceland are good at, siphoning, they started transferring the fuel into the cans we had brought back with us. Our normal protocols told us we should not "borrow" things, but rather purchase them or get them through the national response system. But here we were in a country where the national system was down and there was no way of purchasing fuel. So we had to break protocols because otherwise we could not have gone out into the city again to do the job we came here for.

About the time we filled the first can, a person wearing an Air France shirt comes into the lot. I tried to explain to him using simple English and lot of acting that we needed the fuel in order to rescue people from underneath the rubble.

Instead of throwing us out of the lot or calling the police, he was very glad to hear we had arrived to help people and he actually pointed us towards a barrel filled with fuel. He said we could have as much of it as we needed and we certainly came back over the next couple of days and filled up our cans with this fuel courtesy of Air France. Without it, we would have never rescued the three women out of the Caribbean Supermarket later the same day.

Further reading

- Foundation by Isaac Asimov
- I, Robot by Isaac Asimov

Decision Making: Chapter 23

Thinking Outside the Box

> If I had asked people what they wanted, they would have said faster horses.
>
> **Henry Ford**

Leading with Blinders on

It is very easy to get stuck in a certain way of doing things. If things have worked well in the past, why should we change how we do them?

We base our decisions and actions on our experiences and for many of us we fear what new decisions and new approaches may bring, because they are an unknown quantity. Sticking with what we know therefore may seem like the best approach. Then there are those of us who can't "color within the lines" and have trouble doing things the same way twice.

The problem is that, as we continue to do things the way we always did them, the world evolves around us. New technologies, new methods, new solutions emerge while we continue doing the same thing.

As we deal with the challenges that we face during a crisis, we must be willing to look at new ways of doing things. It may be possible to use these different ways immediately or we may have to deal with the challenge the old way, but make note of the fact that, given a bit more time, we might be able to flush out a more innovative way to deal with the challenge.

Innovation in Times of Crisis

> If your actions inspire others to dream more, learn more, do more and become more, you are a leader.
>
> **John Quincy Adams**

When we hear the term "innovation," most of us think of what happens in the product research and development departments of companies. But innovation can happen anywhere, even within the government as we will see in the next section.

Innovation is the process of developing new solutions that meet requirements in value-added new ways. Innovation differs from improvement in that it refers to the notion of doing something different rather than doing the same thing better.

Being innovative in times of crisis means being open to finding new ways to address the challenges you face during the crisis. While we don't want to introduce complex new ways of doing things in the middle of a crisis, we should be open to simple new ways of solving the problems we face.

Hurricane Sandy and the FEMA Innovation Team

As Hurricane Sandy made landfall on the East Coast of the United States in the fall of 2012, the leadership of the Federal Emergency Management Agency (FEMA) made a bold decision. They decided to form a multi-sector, cross-functional team of people in government, non-profit and international organizations, volunteer groups, businesses and concerned citizens — the whole community, as FEMA calls it. This team would deploy into the worst affected area and come up with innovative ways to address challenges in the massive response and recovery efforts that were starting to take place.

This team, made up of seasoned disaster response experts and community activists, met up in Washington DC and quickly set out to the worst affected areas in New York and New Jersey. Their mandate was simple. Find innovative solutions to issues that were hindering people getting the assistance needed. Bypass red tape where needed and focus on making an impact. A secondary mandate was to identify opportunities for innovation, which could not be implemented immediately, but could be devised and tested before the next hurricane period.

In the words of Rich Serino, the deputy head of FEMA:

> In order to identify the real-time challenges, the team co-located alongside FEMA employees in one of our disaster field offices in New York City. In doing so, they were able to work within FEMA and outside FEMA to identify challenges and fill gaps where necessary. There, they could tap into their networks, be a "fresh set of eyes," and question underlying assumptions. The team is able to accomplish innovation in a number of ways: First and foremost, through always keeping the disaster survivor in mind when working towards and delivering solutions. Second, is by looking for ways to connect government with external groups. And third, is making time to talk regularly and brainstorming without restraint.

The innovation team addressed a number of issues during their two-week deployment in the affected areas. They were able to provide connectivity to both formal and informal response entities quickly using a combination of federal and private resources. They were able to get resources reallocated to serve the population in need better and they were able to streamline an otherwise difficult process for people affected by the disaster.

This new field-based innovation team proved to be a great success that FEMA plans to deploy in future emergencies. International response organizations are now looking at how they can learn from the experiences of FEMA and set up similar teams to deploy in international disaster responses.

Encouraging Out of the Box Thinking

There are a number of steps you can take to encourage out of the box thinking:

1. Think fast – allow your stream of consciousness to pour forth quickly and without reflection.

2. Avoid any criticism – allow yourself the freedom to express anything

3. Don't assume – never assume it has been done before. There is always the possibility of new thoughts, new ideas, and new ways of doing things.

4. Be a non-conformist – don't worry about what others will think.

5. Keep records of your thoughts – you never know which ideas are worth visiting at a later date.

6. Mimic – don't be afraid to build upon the ideas of others.

7. Avoid over-analysis – leave details to later.

8. Question repeatedly – is this the best you can do? Can this be adapted? Is there a workaround? Don't be afraid to ask What if?

Although it is difficult to turn out of the box thinking on and off, then these simple steps will help you encourage it. For additional methods of brainstorming you can look at IDEO's rules for brainstorming.

Further reading

- Lateral Thinking by Edward de Bono
- The Art of Possibility by Rosamund Stone Zander and Benjamin Zander
- Change Directions by Georges Philips
- Zig Zag by Keith Sawyer
- Disrupt! Think Epic. Be Epic by Bill Jensen

SECTION 6

Team Dynamics in a Crisis

The way a team plays as a whole determines its success. You may have the greatest bunch of individual stars in the world, but if they don't play together, the club won't be worth a dime.

Babe Ruth

One of the most critical aspects of being a leader is to be able to keep your team working at their optimal level, no matter how difficult the crisis is that you are going through.

In our mission to Haiti, the thing I am most proud of is that we were 35 people who went there and we came back as a stronger team that was in one piece, both physically and mentally — all 35 of us. Witnessing terrible scenes of death and destruction, it is amazing that we survived intact. In this section, we will look at some of the strategies we used to keep the team going and motivated during those difficult times.

Team Dynamics: Chapter 24

Team Empowerment

The best executive is the one who has sense enough to pick good men to do what he wants done, and self-restraint enough to keep from meddling with them while they do it.

Theodore Roosevelt

You Are Not the Center of the Universe

Being the leader of a team does not mean that you have to do everything yourself. That is exactly the reason why you are a team and not doing this solo. You can divide the tasks among the team members and thereby achieve much more than you could have by yourself.

As a leader it is important for you to delegate details to others and for you to focus on the big issues and the strategic vision. This enables you to fully utilize the power of your team.

As a team leader, you don't have to make all decisions yourself. Just like you can divide and conquer the tasks, then you can also divide the decision-making authority among the team members.

The key to being able to spread the decision-making authority among team members is to have given them values and frameworks to follow. You need to provide clear guidelines on where their authority begins and ends. You also instill them with the values that they should hold true to when they make those decisions.

This empowerment in decision-making allows you to focus on the big issues, while you at the same time can rest assured that the small issues, which usually take much more time to deal with, are being handled in a manner that is in line with how you would have handled them.

You Don't Have to be The Best at Everything

> No man will make a great leader who wants to do it all himself, or to get all the credit for doing it.
>
> **Andrew Carnegie**

As I touched earlier in the book, another key benefit of being able to empower others during a crisis is the fact that you don't have to become best at everything that you need to deal with. You can rely on the expertise of others on your team when it comes to aspects they know better than you.

During our first day of operations in Haiti, we decided to split the team up into two groups. The rescuers and the medical team went into the city towards the Caribbean Supermarket, while the logistics and camp team stayed behind at the airport to set up our base of operations. The deputy team leader and I stayed in the camp, the deputy helping to organize the camp, while I was coordinating things with the United Nation's team that had arrived overnight.

A couple of hours after the team left the airport to head into the city, they had already radioed back with the great news that they had pulled two women out of the rubble, and that they were still trying to locate a third person that they could hear. However, they were missing some equipment from the camp and asked if we could have it delivered to them. Since my role at the base camp had scaled down, I decided I would go with the truck to bring them the equipment.

As I arrived at the supermarket, the on-site commander gave me a brief overview of the situation. He had set up a small command post there in the parking lot. The team was working its way into the rubble from multiple sides, trying to locate clearly where the female they could talk to was lying underneath what used to be a five story building, but was now just one big rubble of concrete.

Many would have expected me to assume control at the location and take over from the on-site commander. But I told him to ignore the fact that I was there. He was in control of the entire operation. I told him he knew 100 times more about urban search and rescue than I would ever learn, so it made total sense for him to be leading the operation.

I told him that my role there was to handle all outside distraction and that if he needed something he should ask me to help get hold of someone who could provide what they needed. I was there to act as the buffer he needed from the outside world, to allow him to put his entire focus on the difficult task at hand.

For the next eight hours, this was the way we ran the operation. He was in charge of how to go about searching for the missing person, he was in charge of the rescue operation and he was in charge of deciding when operations were to come to end. My role was to organize outside assistance, including a dog team from our Spanish colleagues, a technical search team from our US colleagues or an ambulance to be placed on standby.

I also took care of keeping the team at base and our support team in Iceland updated on the situation and answering questions from outside media. The only exception to this was that we assigned one person from the team as a liaison to take care of and explain things to a CNN crew that was broadcasting our rescue live to the world. We knew that the publicity this would generate would be very important to the Icelandic Government, which was funding our response.

The role of the leader isn't always to manage everything that goes on. It is to facilitate and enable those that are better equipped to solve the issues at hand to do their work. As a leader it is your key responsibility to ensure that the team has what they need to do their jobs and to get obstacles out of their way.

Creating the Leaders of Tomorrow

> Outstanding leaders go out of their way to boost the self-esteem of their personnel. If people believe in themselves, it's amazing what they can accomplish.
>
> **Sam Walton**

When I lived in Seattle from 1998-2001 I was member of a search and rescue volunteer team that specialized in manning the various incident management functions required during search and rescue missions in the greater Seattle area.

As an overactive volunteer, I participated in close to 80% of all missions, which meant that, over the three year period, I was part of incident command for close to 250 missions. When I moved back to Iceland in 2001 I joined the regional search and rescue command for the capital area. During that time there was a generation change in the SAR command and I quickly became the most experienced incident manager in the group.

Around the same time I also took on the position as head of the regional SAR command. This normally meant that if I was available for a mission I would become the de-facto incident manager both due to my position and to my extensive experience. This was true for the first 9-12 months, where I would take over as the incident commander if I was in town and available when the call came.

However, I knew that if I continued being the lead of every mission, then I would leave a big gap when I would no longer be part of the regional SAR command. So as part of my succession planning, I helped institute a new program for how we would rotate people into the various incident management positions required during a search and rescue mission.

The more experienced members of the SAR command normally rotated carrying a telephone that they monitored 24/7. This "on-call" person would receive the initial information from the police or the authority reporting the incident. For very small incidents, the on-call person managed it, often from their home, without having to call out the entire SAR command.

For bigger operations, they would mobilize the SAR command and run the operations until the head of the SAR command came to the operation center, in which case the head would assume management of the operation.

Having the most experienced person leading the operation is the traditional way of organizing operations. Instead, we kept the person who was on call as the incident manager and those of us, who might have more experience, simply took on different roles within the incident management system.

For me as the head of the SAR command and the most experienced incident manager, this actually created a variation in my role that enabled me to keep myself passionate about my role much longer than if I had simply kept on being the incident manager all the time.

One key aspect to this approach was that we had mentorship built into the process. Whenever I or any of the other more experienced incident managers saw the person in charge forget to do something or make a decision we were not 100% in agreement about, then we simply asked the person to talk to us outside the emergency operation center for a minute. We would then ask the person why he or she made that particular decision or we might ask him or her to they consider doing something differently. Similarly, if they needed to discuss uncertainties or were unsure what options were available to them, they could ask any of us to have a quick talk outside the center.

This was not us overriding the decision. This was us providing guidance that the person in charge could decide to follow or not. Since this process was well known and well understood, they knew that this was not a negative thing, but rather part of learning to become a top-notch incident manager.

Critical to this approach was that we didn't correct them or question their decision-making in front of the entire team. We did it one-on-one in an environment that had been defined beforehand as being a learning environment, not a disciplinary environment.

I am proud to say that by the time I left the regional SAR command, it was full of very experienced incident managers, all of whom I was very comfortable with running missions of any scale.

Further reading

- Tribal Leadership by Dave Logan, John King, and Halee Fischer-Wright
- Empowerment Takes More Than a Minute by Ken Blanchard, John. P. Carlos, and Alan Randolph
- Great Business Teams by Howard M. Guttman
- Lead & Influence by Mark Fritz
- Leading Self-Directed Work Teams by Kimball Fisher
- Monday Morning Motivation by David Cottrell
- Tribes by Seth Godin

Team Dynamics: Chapter 25

Team Morale

A leader is a dealer in hope.

Napoleon Bonaparte

The Key to Effective Teams

A team's morale affects its effectiveness significantly. If your team morale is high, then they work hard towards solving the challenges in front of them. If your team morale is low, then they give up more easily when faced with difficult challenges. When morale is low they don't think outside the box and don't find solutions to the problems they face.

If your team has in any way been affected by the crisis, then you are bound to have low morale when starting your effort. Their minds will be distracted since they are focused on the challenges they themselves have had to deal with and may not see a way out. It is in these times that you, the crisis leader, need to motivate them with all your abilities. You need to help paint a picture for them that shows the light at the end of the tunnel. You must give them hope and explain to them the crucial role that they will play in solving this crisis.

If, on the other hand, you are leading a team that is being sent in to work on a crisis that does not directly affect you and your team members, then morale is often high because they feel the pride of being asked to help deal with the crisis. This pride, coupled with the feel of contribution, the excitement of going to the crisis area and the vision of themselves as "heroes" coming to help will help keep morale high.

No matter which way it starts out, one of your crucial roles as a leader is to ensure that you keep morale high, even during the most difficult times. Your ability to do that depends on a number of things including:

- **Your rapport with your team members**: Are they open with you? Will they tell you as soon as morale starts going down so you can address the issues before they get out of bounds?

- **Your ability to read others**: Are you able to read the body language and sense the emotional state of people on your team, so that even when they don't tell you something is wrong, you are able to address it?

- **Your ability to understand how the situation is affecting people**: Are you able to analyze the effects that the outside stimuli of the situation around you and your team are having on your team morale?

Keeping Morale High during Mission in Haiti

During the Haiti mission, we put high emphasis on trying to keep morale high. Working in critical conditions where life and death are on the line, the ability of the team to function effectively is crucial. As a team leader, it was important for me to ensure that the team got assigned to tasks that were appropriate for their capability and skillset. Furthermore, it was important that they got teamed up with other teams that were of similar capacity. Having tasks that were challenging but also rewarding helped ensure morale was high.

Even when, at the end of the day, the team had not saved any lives, it became important to make them understand that the work they had done was just as important as if they had saved many lives.

Shielding them from the outside political turmoil while at the same time communicating with them what was happening was also very important. Letting them know that our "back office" team in Iceland was doing a great job of informing and supporting their families was a high boost to morale. Being able to focus on the difficult tasks at hand and not have to worry about what was going on back home allowed them to work very efficiently every day of the mission.

It was important for me as a team leader constantly to get feedback from squad leaders as well as individuals in a team about their perception of morale. I asked them to communicate openly any issues that were affecting morale. One example of this was on the third day of our mission when the team got paired up with a rescue team that was doing their first international response mission.

During the day there were a number of conflicts between the two teams, especially around how and where the teams should be working. As I learnt of these conflicts, I took immediate steps to resolve these issues and prepared myself for talking to the team when they would come back to base. First of all, I got approval from those leading the rescue efforts to put our team in charge of the combined effort since our team was much more experienced than the other team. I then made sure that, the following day, the team would get assigned a very challenging yet rewarding assignment.

I also made sure that they would be teamed up with the best rescue team on site. When the team came back, I first made sure they could vent their frustrations and I promised them I would take that feedback all the way to those in charge. I then told them that I had made sure that this would not happen again and that I would be taking all of their feedback directly to those in charge of the team in question. I told my team that I would make those in charge aware of the lack of capacity this particular team had in working in international disaster environments.

I subsequently told them of the assignment for the following day and also told them that I would be joining them in the field not to lead the rescue effort but rather to ensure there were no issues arising between the two teams.

After speaking with those in charge of the urban search and rescue coordination, it was decided that we would team up the following day with the USA TF-1 team from Fairfax, Virgina. This was a team that ICE-SAR was very familiar with, since it was the team that originally trained ICE-SAR in urban search and rescue.

The following day, we went with USA-TF1 to look for survivors in downtown Port-Au-Prince, the most dangerous part of Haiti to operate in. With strong security support from UN Peacekeepers and US Paratroopers, the two teams worked together as one to search all the collapsed buildings in downtown. That evening the team came back to base tired but feeling very happy about what had been accomplished. The change in morale between the two days was stark.

Factors Affecting Team Morale

To understand team morale better, it is important for you to understand the different factors that can affect it. This section will give you a brief overview of the key factors:

- **Communication/Feedback** - One of the most crucial factors to team morale is how much bidirectional communication exists between leadership and the team. Leaders need to keep team members aware of what is going on and listen to the feedback of the team. If they fail to do so, team members will quickly lose confidence in the leadership.

- **Changes in leadership** - Change of leadership should be avoided during a crisis, unless a leader is incapable of fulfilling their role, since changing the leadership in the midst of the crisis may have a negative effect on team morale.

- **Team member opportunity** - What tasks team members are asked to do has significant effect on morale. If all they get to do are mundane tasks, then morale quickly fades. But, if they are really given the opportunity to employ all of their skills and strengths, or develop new ones, morale will rise.

- **Confidence in leadership** - The more confident team members are in the abilities of their leader, the better the morale. If they start to doubt the abilities of the leadership, morale quickly fades.

- **The nature of the work** - It is important for the team members to feel that the work they are doing is actually making a difference in dealing with the crisis. Even mundane tasks can become rewarding if the leader explains to the team members why that task is important in the big picture.

- **Work load** - Finding good balance between working too much or having too little to do is key to keeping morale high. If people feel like their time is being spent doing nothing or waiting for things to happen, morale quickly fades. Having a lot of work to do is fine as long as people feel they are making a difference.

- **Level of satisfaction** - As long as people feel they are actually making a difference, morale usually stays high. Knowing that the hard work you just performed was meaningful and not a waste of time increases the level of satisfaction the team member gets and that automatically translates into higher morale.

- **Team work** - If the team members are not working well together or if there are clashes between personalities, then morale is affected. It is important for any crisis leader to be on the lookout for these kind of issues and deal with them promptly.

- **Level of supervision** - Too much supervision often results in low morale. Team members want to feel empowered and feel like they have the trust of their leadership to perform the tasks they have been assigned. Micro management is one of the surest ways to kill morale.

- **Self-perception** - How people perceive themselves affects morale. If they have low self-confidence it is difficult to raise their morale.

- **Reward system/image** - We all want to be acknowledged for work well done. When leadership fails to recognize good work, morale is affected. Leaders need to take the time to be on the lookout for work well done and reward it even if simply by verbal acknowledgement in front of other team members.

- **Experience** - The level of experience a team member has is often directly related to their age or education level. This can affect how they perceive the tasks at hand, the environment around them and other outside factors. If people feel the tasks they are being assigned are beneath them and their capabilities, without you acknowledging that you know they are capable of much more, then that will affect morale.

- **Outside factors (family, etc.)** - Dealing with a crisis is difficult enough, but if team members also have to deal with other outside factors such as personal crises at home, their ability to function and concentrate will go down as well as their morale.

Signs of Low Morale

There are a number of cues that can tell you when morale is getting low. Some of these are:

- **Obvious unhappiness** – the way team members act and behave and especially how they say things can be a good sign of unhappiness.

- **Increased complaints about work, or other team members** – if team members start complaining more than usual about the tasks at hand or about their teammates, then this is an obvious sign morale is going down.

- **Increased absenteeism** – if people start avoiding having to come to work, then that is often a sign that they are unhappy and that their morale is low. Absenteeism can often be a symptom of pain avoidance.

- **An increase in conflict between team members** – if tension between team members increases frequently, then morale is going down rapidly. When morale is high, team members are more likely to resolve their disputes in a constructive manner.

- **Insubordination or unruliness** – if team members stop following directions and act on their own, then that is usually a good sign of low morale.

- **Disorganized work environments** – when morale is high team members usually keep their work environment organized so they can perform their tasks more efficiently. As morale goes down the sense of keeping things organized quickly deteriorates.

- **Increased employee turnover** – when morale is low, team members are more likely to leave and look for other work. The more team members that leave the worse the situation is.

- **Decreased productivity** – when morale is low, team members are not as productive. A leader that notices a sharp decline in productivity should investigate if low morale is the cause.

- **Use of alcohol** – when morale goes down, some team members may have the tendency to look towards alcohol or other drugs to numb their dissatisfaction or boredom.

Motivation and Morale

> Leadership is lifting a person's vision to high sights, the raising of a person's performance to a higher standard, the building of a personality beyond its normal limitations.
>
> **Peter Drucker**

Your ability as a leader to motivate your team greatly affects team morale. However, it is important to remember that motivation is all about enabling others to feel better about themselves and what they are doing. By addressing the factors mentioned above you can enable team members to feel better about the work they are doing.

Further reading

- Drive by Daniel H. Pink
- Start with Why by Simon Sinek
- Tribal Warfare in Organizations by Peg C. Neuhauser
- The Servant Leader by James A. Autry
- The Team by Pat Cunningham Devoto
- Soup by Jon Gordon

Team Dynamics: Chapter 26

Dealing with Stress

One of the tests of leadership is the ability to recognize
a problem before it becomes an emergency.

Arnold Glasow

Handling Difficult Situations

Working on a crisis can take its toll on those involved. It is therefore very important to understand how stress affects people and to be on the lookout for increased levels of stress within your team. If left unhandled, stress can develop into severe psychological conditions such as post-traumatic stress disorder (PTSD). As a leader you are responsible for ensuring that stress gets minimized and dealt with.

In this chapter, we will look at some of the most common causes of stress during crisis, discuss the signs of stress and provide some strategies for how to deal with it.

Stress During Crisis

Anyone can hold the helm when the sea is calm.

Publilius Syrus

There are a number of things that can cause stress during a crisis. A few of the most common ones are:

- **Fear of the unknown** – not knowing what lies ahead and whether they are capable of dealing with it causes uncertainty in team members. Uncertainty increases their level of stress.

- **Scenes of devastation** – during crisis we often experience things that are beyond what we have to deal with on a daily basis. Seeing how the crisis affects other human beings and seeing the despair in their eyes severely affects your own emotional state. Both the natural empathic response and not knowing how to deal with it can severely affect any person.

- **Feeling of helplessness** - when the situation is really bad it is easy to feel lack of ability to address the situation in any meaningful way.

- **Your own situation** – if you and/or your family and friends were directly affected by the crisis, your fear of how to deal with your own personal situation can cause high stress.

- **Feeling guilty** – there are a number of ways that you can start feeling guilty in the response of crisis. First of all, you may feel guilt about feeling excited by the opportunity to respond yet the crisis is causing so much harm and despair. Secondly, you may feel guilty over the fact that you are not able to help everyone affected by the crisis. Thirdly, there is survivor guilt; feeling guilty that you are unscathed when others are not. Finally, you may feel guilty about not being able to do more.

If morale is low, stress is also likely to increase, so all of the factors mentioned in the previous chapter can also induce stress if not dealt with properly. As a team leader, it is important for you to address issues of morale and stress hand in hand.

Signs of Stress

It is important for you to be on the lookout for various signs of stress within your team. These include:

- Memory problems
- Inability to concentrate
- Moodiness
- Irritability or short temper
- Feeling overwhelmed
- Poor judgment
- Aches or pains
- Lack of sleep
- Lack of appetite
- Excessive use of alcohol or other drugs
- Isolating from others

Strategies for Dealing with Stress

The better you prepare your team for the difficulties ahead the less stressful the situation will be for them. A good way to reduce the fear of the unknown is to help set expectations correctly before they go out and deal with the crisis.

Every morning in Haiti, it was my role as the team leader to help prepare the team psychologically for the difficult tasks ahead. I would tell them what they might expect to experience and I also told them that it was quite normal for them to be emotionally affected by what they would face. I also emphasized the importance of not burying these emotions within themselves but rather talk about them with their teammates.

I also tried to set their expectations for what work they would need to perform that day. It was important for me to explain clearly to them how those tasks were important in the big picture of things. Knowing that those difficult tasks were important made it easier for them to deal with the difficulties surrounding them.

Furthermore, I would provide them with news from home of how their work was being perceived by their fellow countrymen. Giving them a morale boost by reading aloud some of the headlines about our work in the Icelandic newspapers made them feel like they were doing important work. All of this helped boost their emotional state before taking on the difficulties of that day.

Throughout the mission, the team members had been grouped into pairs into, an approach referred to as the buddy system. In the buddy system, team members who work closely together are teamed up and given the responsibility of monitoring each other's safety, physiological, and psychological state.

Team members would not only ensure that their buddy was drinking enough water and eating enough food but they would also monitor signs of stress in each other. Many situations that could have escalated were simply dealt with by buddies talking openly with each other and discussing each other's emotional state.

When this was not enough, the buddies could bring the situation up to their squad leader or to the team leader. Having emphasized the importance of discussing these things openly throughout our training and then placing strong focus on it in every team meeting during the mission ensured no one was afraid of letting their feelings be known.

Every evening as the team returned to base, my first task was to talk with the squad leaders to get their input on what had happened during the day. I then used that input to speak with the team at large about what had happened to them during the day, allowing individual team members to talk about these things in front of everyone else. I made sure to tell them that the feelings they were experiencing were quite normal and nothing to be ashamed of. I also told them that they were always welcome to talk in private with either me or any of the squad leaders.

After our team meeting, the different squads would go to their respective tents where, in a more informal and personal way they continued the discussions amongst colleagues. This allowed them to put closure to their daily experience.

Even though this process is best applied to already existing teams, then I would suggest following it also for ad-hoc teams that get created in the midst of a crisis. You simply have to put more effort into bringing together the different members of the team.

Formal Processes for Dealing with Stress

Over the decades, ICE-SAR has responded to various emergencies and disasters. However, it is only in the last 10-15 years that a more formal process has been put in place to deal with the effects responding to crisis situations has on the psychological state of our volunteers. Having entire teams almost all burned out after difficult missions taught us the importance of putting the same emphasis on the psychological welfare of our members as we do on their personal safety.

The twice a day meetings were simply the first step in a more formal process that ICE-SAR has in place for addressing the stress inflicted by dealing with difficult situations.

While the team was still deployed in Haiti, families and friends were invited to a session where they were told about how to recognize signs of PTSD in their loved ones as they returned back home after the mission. Although, jokingly, team members referred to this session as a free pass from having to do housework for the first few weeks after returning, the truth was that this session ensured that the buddy system would continue after coming back home because loved ones would help monitor the team member after arrival.

On the way back from Haiti, the team took advantage of a required rest period for the pilots of the plane that picked us up to relax and recharge before returning back home. This stopover, something that is part of our formal process, was used to conduct a formal debrief session where all team members were asked to talk about how the mission had affected them emotionally. This session allowed team members to vent and discuss things openly. The only rules were that no criticism was allowed and that what was being said would not leave the meeting.

After returning home to Iceland, each squad then had a formal and required debrief session led by a crisis counselor from the National Hospital of Iceland. Within the following month, all team members were also required to participate in a one on one session with the same counselor.

Seeing tens of thousands of dead bodies either piled on the streets or up close and personal in collapsed buildings that our team searched through will always stay with every single one of us. I am, however, very proud of the fact that none of the 35 team members who took part in this mission suffered from PTSD or burned out and left their rescue team following this mission. I credit that to the strict focus placed on psychological welfare that ICE-SAR has engrained in all their search and rescue operations.

Further reading

- Who Moved my Cheese? by Kenneth Blanchard
- Why Zebras Don't Get Ulcers by Robert M. Sapolsky
- Adrenaline Fatigue by James L. Wilson
- The PTSD Workbook by Soili Poijula and Mary Beth Williams
- Once a Warrior – Always a Warrior by Charles W. Hoge
- 200 Ways to Calm Down by Antoinette Parekh

SECTION 7
After the Crisis

Any idiot can face a crisis – it's day to day living that wears you out.

Anton Chekhov

Thankfully, all crises will come to an end eventually. As a crisis leader, it is important for you to not just stop everything because the crisis is over. Some of the most important tasks are yet to be done. This includes celebrating work well done, learning from mistakes and focusing on improving the way we deal with future crises, while at the same time bringing about the closure needed by those involved.

After The Crisis: Chapter 27

Celebrate Work Well Done

> It is better to lead from behind and to put others in front, especially when you celebrate victory when nice things occur. You take the front line when there is danger. Then people will appreciate your leadership.
>
> **Nelson Mandela**

Focus on Things that Went Well

In the immediate aftermath, it is important to celebrate work that was done. Team members must have a feeling that all the hard work they put into dealing with the crisis was actually worth the effort. By focusing at this point on what went well, the sense of accomplishment rose.

Of course, there are a number of things that could have gone better. But the time for looking at those in a critical yet constructive manner is not in the immediate aftermath of the crisis. If the focus shifts too soon to addressing those issues, then the good things that were accomplished get forgotten quickly.

It is important for the crisis leader to help all team members to keep this focus. The leader can do so by helping the team tell the story of dealing with the crisis from the positive aspect.

Shining the Spotlight on Your Team

A leader is best when people barely know he exists, when his work is done, his aim fulfilled, they will say: we did it ourselves.

Lao Tzu

As a leader, this is your opportunity to ensure that your team members, who were the ones who did all the hard work, get ample recognition for the great work they did. Too many leaders forget to put the spotlight on their team and end up enjoying all of the attention themselves. This can quickly lead to bad morale moving forward.

For you, it should be reward enough to see your team members enjoy the feeling, the satisfaction of a job well done. You will have ample opportunities to receive your own acknowledgements for the work you did in leading the team through the crisis. The most important acknowledgements will be the ones your own team members will give to you for great leadership in time of crisis. They were the ones who really saw up close the work that you did. Having them acknowledge your work should be more rewarding than any external recognition.

A true crisis leader steps out of the spotlight and shines it upon his team. One important aspect of putting the spotlight on others is watching how you talk about the work that was done. Focus on using the word we instead of I. Talk about the team's accomplishments rather than your own.

Recognize the Efforts of Everyone

Leadership is unlocking people's potential to become better.

Bill Bradley

While it is important to provide that external recognition it is just as important for you as a crisis leader to recognize everyone individually. You should take the time to speak with every team member personally and ensure they feel the sense of accomplishment for the work they did. Again, it is important to make them understand that their contribution was a critical part of the overall big picture. Without having all of the individual components of a team functioning to the best of their ability the team could never have accomplished their overall mission.

Further reading

- The 7 Habits of Highly Effective People by Stephen R. Covey
- Gung Ho! by Ken Blanchard
- Coach Wooden's Greatest Secret by Pat Williams and James D. Denney
- Beyond the Final Score by Tom Osborne

After The Crisis: Chapter 28

Be Critical but Positive

Leadership and learning are indispensable to each other.

John F. Kennedy

We All Make Mistakes

When the dust settles, it is important that we look back at how we dealt with the crisis and identify ways to learn from it. The concept of a perfect response to a crisis is only theoretical. We all make mistakes, especially in chaotic environments and we must recognize that that is normal. The important thing about mistakes is to learn from them and reduce the likelihood of them occurring again. One should look at mistakes as opportunities to learn and we should never stop learning as long as we live.

The Importance of a Formal Process for Learning

True leadership lies in guiding others to success. In ensuring that everyone is performing at their best, doing the work they are pledged to do and doing it well.

Bill Owens

When dealing with the aftermath of a response to a crisis, it is important to have in place a formal process for capturing the learnings. Due to the chaotic nature of crisis it is easy to get distracted and not process these learnings in an organized manner.

It is also important to involve the entire team in the process. There will be a number of learnings that are relevant to the entire team, but there will also be learnings that are relevant to specific roles within the team. It is important that your process ensures that both aspects get addressed.

It is my experience that it is better to start out with identifying the common learnings that are relevant to the team at large and then focus on individual roles. That way there is less duplication of efforts in identifying learnings.

It is also our experience that it is better to keep this process very open and not be afraid of pointing out the more difficult learnings that need to be made. This can be best achieved by laying the ground rule of being critical yet constructive when discussing any potential learning.

Sadly, there have been hundreds if not thousands of lessons-learned documents written that never get acted upon. They should probably more accurately been called lessons-identified documents. In order to really learn, it is important that your process ensures that no lesson is identified, without initiating the action required to really learn from it.

Learning from Haiti

About a month after returning from Haiti, the formal process for capturing the learnings from the mission started. It was kicked off with a team meeting were all those who participated in the mission attended. During this meeting the process was explained and the ground rules put in place.

Before the next meeting team members were asked to identify things that could be improved. These suggestions were then grouped into functional areas. Each functional area was then discussed in further detail in groups consisting of those who were responsible for that functional area.

When each group had agreed upon the issues that were faced, those responsible for the particular functional area were asked to give suggestions for how to improve and learn from those issues. These suggestions were then discussed within the team and, when there was an agreement on the way forward, tasks were assigned to take the first steps towards addressing the issues.

All discussions and decisions were captured into a lessons-learned document and into the overall task list of the team. This ensured that the reasoning for each lesson was properly documented for future team members and leadership. Furthermore, capturing the tasks into the overall prioritized task list ensured that this was not just another lessons-identified document that would collect dust on a shelf.

The overall process from start to finish took over six months. Although this was almost double the time we had planned for the activity, we felt that it was worth the effort and that it was leading to our team becoming even more efficient and better prepared than it was before.

You may not have the luxury of six months to perform a detailed after action review. It is however important that you go through the same steps, even if all you can do is to perform a quick after action meeting, often referred to as "hotwash" by first responders. During the hotwash, you quickly gather the issues identified and put in place action items to dig more deeply into those issues and find ways to avoid them in the future.

Keep Your Focus on Resilience

A good leader is a person who takes a little more than his share of the blame and a little less than his share of the credit.

John Maxwell

As you identify ways to address the issues that you experienced during the crisis, it is important for you always to find ways to make your team better prepared and more resilient to those issues. The best way to deal with an issue is to ensure it cannot happen again. This may require adding skills to your team, changing the way you do things, or organizing your team differently.

You should never be afraid to make changes to the way you do things just because you have always done them a certain way before. If you can find new and innovative ways that make your team more resilient to those issues, then those changes are worthwhile.

Further reading

- Humble Inquiry by Edgar H. Schein
- Leading Change by John P. Kotter
- The Fifth Discipline by Peter M. Senge
- It Worked for Me by Colin Powell
- Chasing Chaos by Jessica Alexander

After The Crisis: Chapter 29

Moving On

The final test of a leader is that he leaves behind him in other men, the conviction and the will to carry on.

Walter Lippman

There Will Always Be Future Crisis

In the humanitarian response community, there have always been disasters that we use to compare everything else to. After the tsunami in south-east Asia in 2004, many responders were caught in the following years comparing future crisis with the Tsunami. The same is true for many of those who responded to Haiti. It is important to remember that both of those crises were outliers and that the next crisis you deal with may not be as big but it is just as important to those affected by it.

We must take each crisis we face as a new and separate challenge. We must understand that each crisis happens within a separate context. The ability of those who are affected to deal with a crisis also evolves and we must be willing to change our approach based on those changes all around us.

Dealing with Change

Leaders think and talk about the solutions. Followers think and talk about the problems.

Brian Tracy

As a crisis leader, you must be willing to continually evolve and adapt to all the changes around you. If you are stuck on doing things "the way we always have done them," then you are likely to become outdated and irrelevant very quickly. A great example of this can be taken from the changes currently affecting the disaster response community.

Just a few years ago, disaster managers would drive all disaster response in a top down manner. They could tell formal response organizations what tasks to do and information about the situation would flow back up the command chain through the same formal responders. Citizens would receive directives from authorities on what to do. They were seen as victims who were not able to do anything except receive assistance.

Improvements in communication technology, especially the explosive growth in mobile phone ownership, and the rise of social media enabled survivors of disasters to communicate their needs more clearly and to organize their own response. This has caused a 180 degree change from a top down approach to a survivor-centric approach.

As crisis leaders, the disaster managers must now respond in a completely new way. They must exercise their ability to listen to, support, and influence survivors instead of exercising their ability to command and control.

You, as a crisis leader, must be willing to evolve continually and adapt yourself to the changing environment around you. You must not fear change but embrace it and use it to achieve your goals in new, innovative and more efficient ways than you were able to before. This will enable you to deal with even more complex crises that you will most certainly face in the future.

Getting Back to Normal

Most of us will experience difficulties in getting back to the normal life after spending days or weeks dealing with a crisis. Getting out of the crisis mode, where everything is driven forward on adrenaline can be quite difficult. Even getting back to normal sleep patterns may take days or weeks.

Being surrounded by family and friends instead of fellow crisis responders can be strange. The family and friends did not experience the same things as you. To them life went on, while you may have experienced life altering moments.

It is important for you to understand that all of these things are normal feelings. You must recognize them and find ways to cope with them. One of the best ways I have found is to find someone to talk to about those things and share your feelings openly with them. They key is not to lock all of these feelings in, but to openly acknowledge them and deal with them.

Remember that even Superman has to cope with being Clark Kent.

Further reading

- Where You Left Me by Jennifer Gardner Trulson
- An Unbroken Bond by Edie Lutnick
- Focus on the Good Stuff by Mike Robbins

Afterword

There comes a time in your life when your focus shifts from success to significance.

Edward G. Happ

Throughout my close to twenty years of volunteering and working for non-profit organizations, I have had the honor of leading some great teams of people who all shared the common goal of doing something good for others. In my mind, as a leader, your role is not to direct those people or to manage them. In my mind, as a leader, your role is to help them build that shared vision and then do everything you can to eliminate any obstacle they may face in achieving that shared vision.

This is particularly true when you lead a team through a crisis, such as when responding to a large-scale natural disaster. During those times, your task as a leader is to keep your team focused on the task and help shield them from all the distractions that are all around such as media, humanitarian politics, and other operational issues. Furthermore, your task during those difficult times is to ensure that the morale of the team and the individual wellbeing of each team member are high, so that they can deal with the difficult tasks at hand.

To be given an opportunity to lead teams of great people in difficult times that are all focused on helping their fellow human beings is a great honor and privilege. At one point in my life, I was offered to go back into a highly paid job in software development after having worked for a few years in the humanitarian world. The decision to continue working on helping other people in need was a simple one. My life's focus had shifted from success to significance as Ed so nicely put it.

What is it that draws people into this world? It is certainly not the complex international and organizational politics, which hamper progress. It is certainly not the adrenaline of operating in dangerous environments. For me it is that smile on a person's face, once you know you have made a difference in her life. In her beautiful song to the humanitarian community, the singer Beyoncé, put it very well. She talked about leaving a footprint on this earth, a mark that said "I Was Here."

The late author and visionary Stephen Covey also put it very clearly when he said, "the need to leave a legacy is our spiritual need to have a sense of meaning, purpose, personal congruence, and contribution." His definition of the need to leave a legacy fits very much with my own sense of purpose. For many people, leaving a legacy means having "monuments" that they can point to and say, "I did that." For many people, leaving a legacy means becoming popular, talked about or even famous. For many people, leaving a legacy means achieving certain titles or positions of power.

However, for me, leaving a legacy is about knowing that I made a difference in people's lives. It is about knowing that those that I worked with felt they were better people because they knew me. It is about knowing that those people that my team and I tried to help felt they were better off because we helped them. It is about knowing that things may be done better in the future because of some work that my team and I have done.

As a leader, it is also your role to ensure that your team feels that their legacy is growing when being part of the team. Sadly, too often, we see conflict arise within teams or organizations because people feel that other team members are "claiming the success" of the team effort. However, a true leader knows that nothing ever is achieved only by an individual. It is the whole of the team, which creates the result. A true leader therefore tries to ensure that all team members, no matter what their role, understand that their effort was a key part of the integral effort required to achieve the common goal. Together the team leaves a footprint saying "We Were Here."

Throughout this book, I have given you an insight into what makes a better crisis leader. I hope that you have enjoyed the trip we took together and that you have learned something during that trip. It is my hope that you have discovered your need to develop and stay true to your principles. That you will plan and prepare for the crisis ahead, but remember to expect change to occur.

It is my hope that you will be open to opportunities that lie ahead and that you are prepared to be wrong. Finally that you have understand the importance of a successful team, that you remember to listen to your team, listen to advice of the people, yet make decisions from your heart. Do this and you will succeed in being a good crisis leader.

In closing, I want to quote one of my favorite authors, Robin Sharma, with the best advice he ever got, which was from his father. This advice based on the old Indian saying states:

> "When you were born, you cried and the world rejoiced.
> Live your life in such a manner that when you die, the
> world cries and you rejoice."

Printed in Great Britain
by Amazon

58837487R00102